Why Medieval Philosophy Matters

WHY PHILOSOPHY MATTERS

Series editor: Professor Constantine Sandis, University of Hertfordshire, UK

Why Philosophy Matters focuses on why a particular philosopher, school of thought, or area of philosophical study really *matters*. Each book will offer a brief overview of the subject before exploring its reception both within and outside the academy and our authors will also defend different provocative outlooks on where the value of philosophy lies (or doesn't, as the case may be). *Why Philosophy Matters* is accompanied by an ongoing series of free events (talks, debates, workshops) in Bloomsbury. Podcasts of these events will be freely available on the series page.

Books in this series

Why Iris Murdoch Matters, Gary Browning

Also available from Bloomsbury

Medieval Philosophy: A Multicultural Reader, Bruce Foltz
Technic and Magic, Federico Campagna

Why Medieval Philosophy Matters

STEPHEN BOULTER

BLOOMSBURY ACADEMIC
LONDON • NEW YORK • OXFORD • NEW DELHI • SYDNEY

BLOOMSBURY ACADEMIC
Bloomsbury Publishing Plc
50 Bedford Square, London, WC1B 3DP, UK
1385 Broadway, New York, NY 10018, USA

BLOOMSBURY, BLOOMSBURY ACADEMIC and the Diana logo are trademarks of Bloomsbury Publishing Plc

First published in Great Britain 2019

A catalogue record for this book is available from the British Library.

A catalog record for this book is available from the Library of Congress.

ISBN: HB: 978-1-3500-9415-4
PB: 978-1-3500-9416-1
ePDF: 978-1-3500-9417-8
eBook: 978-1-3500-9418-5

Series: Why Philosophy Matters

Typeset by Deanta Global Publishing Services, Chennai, India
Printed and bound in Great Britain

To find out more about our authors and books visit www.bloomsbury.com and sign up for our newsletters.

CONTENTS

Preface vi

Introduction: Why philosophy matters 1
1 Scholasticism and common sense 25
2 Scholasticism and the sciences 45
3 The meta-philosophy of scholasticism 69
4 Scholasticism on the various kinds of distinction 89
5 The scholastics and arguments for the existence of God 111
6 Scholasticism and Western 'disenchantment' 135

Notes 153
Epilogue 174
Some useful Latin terms and phrases for philosophers 177
Appendix I: When were the Middle Ages 183
Bibliography 191
Index 197

PREFACE

A new approach

Philosophers with a special interest in medieval thought have spent much time and effort expounding the virtues of scholastic principles to other professionals in the discipline. Indeed, it might appear that specialists in medieval philosophy have been doing little else since serious work began on the project of recovering the thought of the scholastics well over a century and a half ago. Our collective endeavours have continually been straining in the same direction – making the case for medieval philosophy to the philosophical mainstream. So why yet another work on why medieval philosophy matters? Surely if there is a case to be made for medieval philosophy it has been made by now.

There is a sense in which this is right, and another in which it is wrong. It is right insofar as medieval specialists have been particularly adept at showing how familiarity with scholastic thought can help the contemporary philosopher address highly specialized issues of ongoing concern in metaphysics, epistemology, philosophy of mind and ethics. Moreover, a significant body of work has been produced which shows that the roots of early modern philosophy – a period with which the philosophical mainstream is familiar – lie deep within scholasticism itself. This two-pronged approach, philosophical and historical, has been popular amongst medieval specialists seeking to establish a dialogue between scholastic and contemporary philosophy.

Regrettably these efforts have had little impact on the philosophical mainstream. It had been hoped that the landmark publication in 1982 of *The Cambridge History of Later Medieval Philosophy* would inaugurate a new period in which contemporary philosophers would no longer work in ignorance of medieval achievements. But as John Marenbon notes in his introduction to

The Oxford Handbook of Medieval Philosophy of 2012, these hopes have largely failed to materialize. Medieval philosophy remains a minority interest within the profession, with many philosophy departments still having no specialist on staff.

In retrospect it is easy to see that our hopes were misplaced. It is not just that philosophers entertain the usual suspicions of things medieval, although this is a significant factor. Just as important is the current state of the discipline. As with virtually all subjects, philosophy has become increasingly specialized, and those working in one domain rarely have anything to say to those working in another. But more than this, the discipline as a whole has fragmented into isolated camps with distinct self-images, agendas, projects and methodologies. These very different understandings of the philosophical enterprise compromise the prospects of meaningful dialogue amongst contemporary philosophers themselves. In such an environment it was always going to be difficult to win a ear for an alien medieval voice.

There is therefore an important sense in which the case for medieval philosophy has yet to be made, if we understand this to mean finding a way to make the case resonate with non-specialists. But the *Why Philosophy Matters* series provides the occasion for considering a different way to champion medieval philosophy. This series is a response to the growing impression abroad in society at large that philosophy *as a discipline* is redundant. This series calls on philosophers to push back against this redundancy thesis. Now I maintain that it is in confronting *this* challenge that medieval and contemporary philosophy can make common cause. The overarching thesis of this book is that those familiar with scholastic thought are uniquely well placed to make the case for philosophy within the wider intellectual community precisely because the scholastic understanding of the discipline, along with its fundamental principles and methodologies, will resonate with those who entertain doubts about the usefulness of philosophy. My hope, then, is to win a new audience for medieval philosophy on the basis that it is uniquely well positioned to show why philosophy itself is anything but redundant. As the discipline continues to come under attack from without, making the case for philosophy matters, and scholasticism can help.

A word of warning is in order. The focus on philosophy's external relations with other disciplines and society at large makes for an unusual book on medieval thought. There are more orthodox ways in which one might try to show that medieval philosophy matters, and these are worth pointing out if only to underline the fact that the case made in this book is only one way to champion the period. Perhaps the most obvious way is to assert that *all* periods of history matter, and so medieval history matters as well. And since the period is standardly taken to span a thousand years (from 500 to 1500), and to have marked the transition from the ancient to the modern world, it would be very odd if nothing of importance had happened in this period. This is the route taken by some intellectual historians. Another approach is to focus on showing how medieval thought can help the contemporary philosopher deal with contemporary internal problems. Here the idea is to establish that a contemporary philosopher can treat medieval thinkers as worthy colleagues. The contemporary school of analytical Thomism is an obvious example of this approach. A third takes issue with the first two. There is a school of thought popular with some medieval specialists which insists that there is little point trying to recover medieval thought for the benefit of contemporary philosophers. According to this school medieval philosophy is so different from contemporary philosophy that there can be no fruitful dialogue between the two. It is not even clear if we can recover what the medieval figures were saying: so different was their mode of thought. On this view the best we can do is merely enjoy the difference of the 'other' in contemplating them. If medieval philosophy matters, it is only because appreciating their 'difference' can bring our own, perhaps unrecognized, assumptions into the light.

While all of these approaches have their merits, I have not adopted them here. There are plenty of good histories available already, and many highly professional works linking medieval and contemporary thought. What is missing is a book which outlines a case for the importance of medieval thought to matters of general interest, and to the pressing matter of philosophy's relation to the wider intellectual world. This is why I have tried to connect aspects of the medieval scholastic framework to issues of general concern, to things that clearly do matter, or ought to matter, to the general reader.

Needless to say, the results of this outward facing orientation will not be to everyone's taste. For in this context the interest of a philosophical insight, method, theory or thinker is no longer judged simply by criteria internal to the discipline, but also, and crucially, by concerns arising from our being situated within a wider social context. This means that much material that would normally be included within a study of medieval philosophy will not find a place here. And much standard fare will be recast in an unusual light in order to bring out its relevance to a non-specialist audience. Moreover, much material that would not normally figure in such a work will be given pride of place. Therefore, this book should *not* be seen as an introduction to medieval philosophy if introductions are meant for readers who *already* have an interest in a given subject and want to know more about it. This book is more of an apology inasmuch as it is an attempt to explain why non-specialists should take an interest in medieval philosophy in the first place. I will have succeeded if a reader decides, upon finishing this book, to pick up one of the many excellent introductions to medieval philosophy patiently awaiting the readers they deserve.

I begin in Introduction by setting out a series of issues that are likely to resonate with the general public, issues that have a distinctly philosophical dimension. These include the redundancy thesis with respect to philosophy as a discipline, the insufficiency thesis with respect to the sciences and a series of aporia that emerge at the level of the social order. These issues are likely to be of interest to an alert reader of any academic background. Moreover, and crucially for my purposes, the logical shape of these issues, that is, their aporetic nature, means that they are amenable to the philosophical mindset and methodology of scholasticism.

Chapters 1 and 2 drive home the point that scholastic thought is very much at ease with both common sense and the sciences. For all the unfamiliarity of this distant period, the metaphysics of the scholastics is very much the implicit metaphysics of the intelligent layperson as well as being the background against which scientific study of the world makes sense. Again, this brings medieval thought into contact with the intuitions and concerns of the general reader.

This preparatory work complete, Chapter 3 then sets out the scholastic project of Faith seeking Understanding. Insofar as this project takes on the task of reconciling individually compelling but contradictory lines of thought, it mirrors the logic of the problems set out in Introduction. If the problems of Introduction were compelling, then the scholastic project itself will no longer appear remote and alien.

Chapter 4 then outlines one of the features of scholastic thought that is both central to that project and of enduring value. Regaining the scholastic material on the nature of distinctions is vital for contemporary metaphysics. But it also set the groundwork for dealing with Moore's historically important Open Question Argument, an argument which lies at the heart of many of the aporia mentioned in Introduction.

Chapter 5 is devoted to showing that a prima facie weakness of scholasticism from a modern, secular point of view, that is, its connection with theology, is not the problem it is often thought to be. Indeed, two scholastic arguments for the existence of God are discussed which should prove useful to contemporary metaphysicians concerned to establish that there is an ontologically basic level to reality.

Finally, in Chapter 6 I return to the aporia regarding the social order sketched in Introduction. In this concluding chapter I set out a scholastic framework for dealing with Weberian disenchantment. Reconnecting our cognitive with our political and economic orders is the main order of business here, and this is shown to be possible by replying on material presented in previous chapters.

The central theme of the book then is that philosophy in general matters because the sciences cannot answer all important questions. Some of these questions arise within the sciences themselves, and some arise at the level of the social order itself. These distinctly philosophical questions, however, are most perspicuously addressed by scholastic metaphysical principles. This is why medieval philosophy in particular matters beyond the halls of academe.

Introduction: Why philosophy matters

This introductory chapter is devoted to explaining why philosophy in general matters to society at large. This means confronting the redundancy thesis, that is, the view that the sciences can address all meaningful questions, and so there is no call for a discipline like philosophy. The key claim of this chapter is that the redundancy thesis is false: there are certain kinds of problems that cannot be addressed by the sciences, questions that fall to a second-order discipline. Many of these problems have their provenance in the sciences themselves. But to illustrate how philosophy in general matters beyond the halls of academe I show that these problems also emerge in areas of public concern, that is, in the fabric of our social order itself. A philosophy that matters is one that can address these problems. Such a philosophy is found in the medieval scholastics.

Introduction

This book is an extended attempt to explain why medieval philosophy matters to anyone interested in grappling with the myriad intellectual and moral challenges facing contemporary society. The most pressing of these challenges are of a distinctly philosophical nature, and they are *not* amenable to treatment by the methods of other disciplines. This is why philosophy in general matters. But I will be at pains to show that the philosophical framework best placed to deal with these contemporary challenges was developed by the scholastic philosophers and theologians of the Middle Ages. This is why medieval philosophy in particular matters.

The first step in the development of my case for medieval philosophy is to establish that there is in fact a need for philosophy. Period. After all, if there is no call for philosophy of any description, then, a fortiori, there is no call for medieval philosophy. So I begin by examining the claim that there is no need for a discipline like philosophy at all because there are no serious questions that cannot be handled by some science or another. Examining this 'redundancy thesis' will serve to bring out the distinctive nature of philosophical problems, and will take up the bulk of this chapter. This preparatory work is crucial because it is only when the logical shape of these problems is made plain that we begin to get an inkling of what a philosophy that matters might look like. A philosophy that matters will be a philosophy that can handle precisely these kinds of problems. In subsequent chapters I will go on to show that such a philosophy is to be found in the scholastics.

Now because consideration of the general must precede consideration of the particular, the formal introduction of the scholastics and their shared philosophical framework and general project is delayed until the opening sections of Chapter 4. Nonetheless, before beginning my case in earnest it is worth pausing to say something about the eventual heroes of our story. In particular it is important to be clear about the meanings of the terms 'medieval', 'scholastic' and 'scholasticism' as I will be using them here.

The term 'medieval' is generally used to refer to a particular historical period, roughly from the fall of the Roman Empire to the beginning of modernity. Traditionally this historical period was taken to span the years 500–1500 AD.[1] Now as it happens, most of the towering figures of scholasticism lived and worked within this historical period, and so they are often thought of as medieval philosophers – hence the use of 'medieval' in the title of this book. But not all scholastics were medieval in this historical sense of the term. So it is important to understand that for our purposes I will use 'scholasticism' and 'scholastic' as terms for a particular intellectual project rather than a time period. Broadly construed, the project is the attempt to synthesize Faith and Reason, which, for the significant majority of scholastics, meant reconciling the theology of Augustine with the philosophy of Aristotle. Thus one counts as a 'scholastic' in my preferred sense if one accepts both Augustine and Aristotle as authorities in their respective domains, and one believes that a fruitful 'dialogue' can be had between the two. Aquinas, Scotus, Buridan, Ockham, Cajetan, Vitoria, Suarez – these are quintessentially scholastic figures. And in terms of influence on the subsequent trajectory of Western philosophy, these scholastic figures were the most significant of the medieval philosophers.

But not all thinkers of the Middle Ages accepted the outlines of this project. Some refused to recognize the authority of Augustine or of any other theologian. Others baulked at Aristotelian metaphysics. Still others were far from convinced that Reason could bring anything to Faith, or Faith to Reason. Many such thinkers had interesting things to say, and a complete account of medieval philosophy in the historical sense would require much space than I have available to me here.[2] A book of this size must have a more restricted aim, and so I will be making a case for the medieval scholastics, as opposed to the entire corpus of medieval philosophical thought.

But all this must wait until we have drawn the essential lessons from an examination of the redundancy thesis.

Squaring up to the redundancy thesis

It has always been easy to doubt the importance of philosophy. Indeed philosophy and philosophers have been easy targets from the very beginnings of the discipline. We have had to defend ourselves from political elites, whose authority may be threatened by our musings on the nature of society and legitimate political authority; we have had to defend ourselves against allegations of undermining religious faith and traditional piety, charges brought by powerful religious bodies; and we have had to defend ourselves from the disparagement of the ordinary man in the street, who seldom understands the niceties of philosophical dialectics. What unites these challenges, however, is the element of unintended flattery about them. If political and religious powers attack us, does this not mean that we have influence, and therefore significance? And if the philosophically untutored ridicule us, does this not merely serve to throw our intellectual sophistication into ever sharper relief? Backhanded compliments like these philosophers can handle.

But what philosophers do not welcome is a challenge to the dignity of the discipline. The redundancy thesis is such a challenge. The redundancy thesis is the claim that society can do without philosophy because there are no important questions that cannot be answered by another discipline, usually some science or another. There might be pseudo-questions that philosophers can clear away, but if a question is significant, if it matters, then, rest assured, there is no need to call a philosopher. Ironically, the redundancy thesis has enjoyed significant support in certain philosophical circles, particularly in the first half of the twentieth century. Of course very few outside of philosophy departments ever paid much attention. But when scientists raise doubts about the value of philosophy, when prominent figures like Stephen Hawking and Leonard Mlodinow say 'Philosophy is dead', and that 'scientists have become the bearers of the torch of discovery in our search for knowledge', people listen.[3] Of course this just adds insult to injury.

The *Why Philosophy Matters* series is a concerted attempt to address the spread of the redundancy thesis within society at large. This particular contribution to the series focuses on the value of medieval philosophy, a much neglected and unfashionable field even within philosophy itself. Now it might be thought a thankless task to advocate on behalf of such a field if even philosophers themselves are unsure of it. But this is largely due to the profession's own unfamiliarity with what is often forbidding and difficult work. Be that as it may, my case for medieval philosophy begins with a preliminary case for philosophy in general. It is only when we see why philosophy in general might matter that a case for medieval philosophy, and scholasticism in particular, becomes feasible. And this means that a defence of medieval philosophy must begin by squaring up to the redundancy thesis.

Sadly there is quite a lot to be said for the redundancy thesis. It is hard to claim that philosophy matters when its social function and its role within the general intellectual economy have been usurped by the far more successful sciences. Hawking and Mlodinow are quite right to say that philosophy is no longer the torch bearer in our quest for knowledge. When we want to know something about the fundamental structure of reality, do we not go to physics and chemistry? When we want to know something about the nature of human beings and the nature of the human mind, do we not go to biology, psychology and the various cognitive sciences? When we want to know something about the social order, its economic, social and political structures, do we not go to the various social sciences? And when we move beyond matters of knowledge to questions about what we ought to do – for example, when we want advice on what environmental policies to pursue, what medicines and procedures we ought to fund on the NHS, whether it is safe to eat GM foods – again, do we not place ourselves in the hands of the scientists, and plough our resources into research and development projects of a scientific nature? Of course we do.

But – surprising as this might sound coming from a philosopher – all of this is as it should be. It would be foolhardy in the extreme *not* to rely on the sciences in these ways, for the sciences have proved to be the most successful intellectual project ever undertaken by human beings. And the benefits in terms of the improved quality of life the sciences now afford clinch the case for the sciences as the leaders in our search for knowledge. So there is indeed something to the view that philosophy as a discipline has gone the way of theology. At one stage in our history theology was the standard bearer. With the advent of the Enlightenment, and when the sciences were still in their infancy, the standard was passed to philosophy. But now that the sciences have found their feet to such brilliant effect, philosophers are relegated to the bench next to the theologians.

What is particularly worrying now – to continue the sporting metaphor – is that philosophers are not even the first pick from the bench. When the sciences fail us, do we seek out a good old-fashioned philosopher, or engage in philosophical reflection ourselves? Rarely. We are far more likely to reach for the exotic fare of 'new age' religions or 'alternative' world views. Even more worryingly, we are increasingly tempted to give up on the very idea of experts in *any* field of enquiry. But if philosophy can't get a game when the first stringers are injured, it is hardly surprising that otherwise intelligent and well-informed people begin to wonder what philosophers and philosophy departments are for.

And again, sad as it is to say, this wonder frequently *increases* after taking a few introductory philosophy courses at university. For the *point* of philosophy is not obvious, and lecturers seldom address this matter in a timely fashion. To make matters worse, the information vacuum is frequently filled by intellectual dilettantes whose interests are limited to ideologically motivated 'social critique', 'transgressing boundaries' or meditations on popular culture. This only gives succour to the redundancy thesis amongst serious people. Indeed, anyone still paying attention is likely to turn away in disgust and hope for the demise of philosophy itself.

But this would be a mistake. A natural mistake, to be sure, but a mistake nonetheless. And it is a mistake because the redundancy thesis is false. The redundancy thesis is false because there are questions that cannot be addressed, let alone answered, by the sciences. Moreover, these are not pseudo-questions of mere academic interest, nor are they confined to the great imponderables like the meaning of Life, Death and the cosmos. Our answers to these questions form the (usually unnoticed) backdrop against which we live our lives, individually and collectively, a backdrop that makes our lives intelligible and bearable. As we shall see, these questions are strictly philosophical in nature. The pressing nature of these questions is ultimately why philosophy matters.

Now my case for philosophy in general, and eventually for medieval philosophy in particular, rests on an account of the nature of philosophical questions. This means that an extended detour into the philosophy of philosophy is necessary before I can begin to set out the principal case of this book. It is only when we recognize that there are strictly philosophical questions that reach into the very fabric of the social order itself, and that these questions are not amenable to treatment by scientific methodologies, that we can get a sense of what a discipline like philosophy is for. And it is only when one has a clear grasp of the logical structure of such questions that one will be in a position to see why the scholastics in particular deserve our very close attention.

What is a philosophical question?

To the philosophical layperson philosophy is the discipline that deals with the so-called 'Big Questions' – the origins of the cosmos, the meaning of life, the meaning of death, whether there is a God, what we can know, what we can hope for, the nature of right and wrong, the good life for human beings and so forth. Now there *is* a sense in which all of these questions are philosophical. Philosophers have weighed in on these issues from time immemorial. But these questions are *not* the preserve of philosophers alone, and so these questions are *not* philosophical per se. In fact philosophy shares these Big Questions with both religion and the sciences. Religion, philosophy and the sciences, when taken in their totality, have historically had a common goal, namely, the provision of a coherent picture of the fundamental structure of reality, of humanity's place within that reality, what we can know of it and ourselves, a picture that then informs how we ought to conduct our lives. One cannot afford to overlook this common ground if one is to properly appreciate the nature of these distinct enterprises.[4]

The main differences between religion, philosophy and the sciences are not so much about ends but about the means to achieve those ends. This is why religion, philosophy and the sciences are often portrayed as being in competition, and hence in mutually antagonistic relationships. Most religions, for example, allow for belief formation processes that are ruled out by philosophers and scientists (e.g. appeals to authority, revelation, an emphasis on faith or personal experience or the importance of ritual). The same applies to the differences between science and philosophy: the former insists that scientifically respectable beliefs are those tested against experience in accordance with scientific method, while the latter allows houseroom for much a priori speculation, conceptual analysis, thought experiments, appeals to ordinary language and other 'intuitions', not simply to spark thoughts and suggest lines of investigation but as ways to defend an answer to a set question.

Of course one should not assume that these belief formation processes are incompatible, that is, that once you've employed a process associated with one enterprise that this forecloses on your being able to employ those of another. This is particularly so in the case of philosophy and the sciences. In fact the picture of philosophy I will develop here is one of a co-operative venture, where both the sciences and philosophy with their respective methodologies make their own distinctive and indispensable contribution to the answering of the Big Questions. Understanding the nature of their respective contributions is key to understanding both.

Now it is relatively clear why the contribution of the sciences is necessary and vital on this project. The sciences, and the methods they employ, are deemed to be competent to address issues in their various empirical domains. This recognized competency is why the various sciences are our first port of call for information regarding these domains when we seek to address the Big Questions. What is not immediately obvious is the role of philosophy. If the sciences are indeed competent in all empirical domains, what aspects of reality remain for the philosopher qua philosopher to investigate?[5] Is philosophy relegated to investigating *non*-empirical reality, whatever that might be?

Certainly many philosophers in the twentieth century have thought as much. The logical positivists, the early and later Wittgenstein, the ordinary language philosophers – to name only a few prominent streams of twentieth-century thought – maintained that the investigation of empirical reality *is* the sole preserve of the sciences, and that philosophy must find something else to do if it is to avoid redundancy. So it was proposed that philosophers ought to focus on the *conceptual frameworks* in which scientific and other discourses are carried out. Languages, natural and formal, became a focus of sustained attention, as analysis of these languages was thought to lay bare the fundamentals of conceptual schemes or frameworks. Thought, concepts, words and languages – rather than things – became the philosopher's object of study. But the focus on thought and language was only one option. Some philosophers took to investigating the nature of *value*. According to the positivists, value, along with good and bad, right and wrong, is not a feature of empirical reality but is a projection of our subjective attitudes. So the development of anti-realist meta-ethics was deemed a respectable philosophical endeavour, as was working out the consequences of such a meta-ethic in political and ideological critiques of the structures of society. Then in the last quarter of the twentieth century philosophers rediscovered a taste for metaphysics. This threw up another list of non-empirical entities to investigate, like possibilities and other modal properties, abstract objects, time and space. Finally, many philosophers effectively gave up on philosophy per se and retreated to the study of the history of the discipline, becoming specialists in the history of ideas.[6]

Much stimulating work was produced investigating non-empirical reality and the history of ideas. But the decision to focus exclusively on the non-empirical was a fateful error. It served merely to re-enforce the thrust of the redundancy thesis as far as the general public was concerned, for it was always unclear what the value of such studies might be to those not primarily concerned to keep philosophers in full-time paid employment. More seriously, the excessively deferential attitude to the sciences that lies behind much twentieth-century philosophical activity re-enforced lines of thought that lie behind what Weber called Western 'disenchantment'. Weber's assessment of the root of Western society's malaise will occupy our attention later. For now the important point is that this fateful error was unforced. Philosophers in the first half of the twentieth century ceded ground to the sciences far too quickly because it was not yet clear to all just how much scientific activity depends on philosophical assumptions. Things have changed. It is now more widely understood that there *is* a vital role for philosophy in the project of providing a coherent account of empirical reality and our place in it, for the sciences cannot do this on their own. It is important to understand why.

The first argument for what I will call 'the insufficiency of the sciences' is perhaps the easiest to grasp. In effect the claim is that the sciences do not provide answers to the Big Questions in any straightforward fashion because the sciences do not as yet agree amongst themselves on fundamental matters. There simply is no monolithic scientific world view. While there might very well be a monolithic *mindset* shared by most scientists, this is not matched at the level of theories. As DeLanda puts it,

> There is no such thing as Science ... [We should] replace Science with a *population of individual scientific fields*, each with its own concepts, statements, significant problems, taxonomic and explanatory schema. There are, of course, interactions between fields, and exchanges of cognitive content between them, but that does not mean that they can be fused into a totality in which everything is inextricably related. There is not even a discernable convergence towards a grand synthesis to give us hope that even if the population of fields is highly heterogeneous today, it will one day converge into a unified field. On the contrary, the historical record shows ... an overall divergent movement.[7]

The point here is that the sciences offer many mature theories, each with impressive empirical credentials; but in many cases they appear to contradict each other.[8] Which science, then, is one to believe? If each of two contradictory theories is empirically adequate, how does one decide in a principled fashion which theory to accept and which to abandon?

It is important that the point of the previous paragraph be properly understood. Under no circumstances should the tensions between the various sciences be taken to imply that the sciences can be ignored. This would be to foolishly overlook the conspicuous success the sciences have enjoyed, and the stupendous improvements they have afforded to standards of living. Rather, the point is that these tensions do not look like they are resolvable simply by gathering more empirical information, that is, by running more experiments and doing more science. Science itself cannot resolve tensions like these. The challenge, rather, is to *re-conceptualize* our theories and their supporting empirical data so as to see how all of them (or most of them, if we are lucky) can be true simultaneously. And if no such re-conceptualization is possible, then we need a principled means of deciding which theories to save and which to reject. Now in actual practice, many proceed chauvinistically as though there is a non-arbitrary hierarchy of scientific authority, with physics given precedence over chemistry and biology, while these are privileged over, say, linguistics and psychology. But it is not clear that any such hierarchy can be justified on purely empirical grounds.

It is precisely here that philosophy enters the picture. Taking up the challenge of rethinking our prima facie incompatible theories and commitments, the better to understand how they can all find their place in a coherent account of reality, is the business of philosophy per se. Handling tensions between respectable lines of thought from first-order disciplines is philosophy's distinctive contribution to the grand project. The primary material that philosophy uses to construct an account of reality comes from the various first-order sciences and common sense. The role of strictly philosophical reflection is to treat the co-ordination problems that arise from (a) the clashes between the various sciences themselves, (b) the clashes between the sciences and common sense, and ultimately, (c) the clashes that arise in the sphere of action arising from contradictory prima facie duties, duties grounded in what we think we know about reality. It is the existence of such aporias, a technical term for co-ordination problems, that justifies the existence of philosophy as a distinct discipline.[9] If there were no such problems, there would be no call for philosophy.[10]

There are two further technical arguments for the insufficiency thesis. Both of these arguments give reasons for maintaining that the sciences are not able on their own to provide answers to first-order questions *even in their respective domains*. The first runs as follows: It was a common place amongst positivists to maintain that the sciences investigate *actual* empirical reality, that is, that which is in fact the case, while philosophers investigate how things *must* be or *could* be or *could never* be. The idea here is that the sciences rely, ultimately, on observation, and while observation reveals how the world actually is, it cannot tell you how it might have been, or could be, or had to be, or could never be. These non-empirical *modal* properties of reality are standardly taken to require distinct non-scientific methods of investigation. In the twentieth century the most common methods of investigating the modal properties of reality consisted of thought experiments which trade on our abilities to conceive how things might turn out in particular unrealized circumstances. That is, the necessary, the possible and the impossible were thought to be closely connected to what we can and cannot *imagine* without running into a *logical* contradiction. But if the modal properties of reality *do* fall outside the remit of the sciences, then it looks as though the sciences are *not* self-sufficient even in their own domains. Why not?

Because of a curious and often overlooked feature of observation, say a particle physicist wishes to establish the existence of a certain kind of theoretical particle. The standard approach would be to look for empirical evidence of such a particle, the idea being that such evidence, if it can be found, would support the claim that the particle exists. But, and this is the crucial point, the empirical evidence that scientific experiments and observation turn up will count in favour of the actual existence of the particle in question *only* if it has been established independently that such a particle is possible. But modalities fall outwith the remit of the sciences, for these investigate the actual, not the modally qualified world. Modalities, on the standard view, fall to metaphysics. So the sciences need strictly philosophical assumptions to operate even in their respective domains.[11]

A second technical argument for denying the insufficiency thesis is less reliant on modal niceties. It runs as follows: we can expect the sciences to provide information about reality only if there are good reasons to believe that mature scientific theories are at least approximately true representations of some aspect of reality. But again it is not clear that this attitude vis-à-vis any scientific theory can be warranted in the absence of extra-empirical commitments. For as Duhem pointed out long ago, it is impossible, strictly speaking, to determine the truth-value of a scientific theory if one relies solely on empirical evidence and logic. This is the so-called 'under-determination of theory by data' problem in the philosophy of science. The logic of verification and falsification is such that whenever an experiment throws up an unexpected result (a 'recalcitrant observation') the scientist need not reject the theory being tested. Of course it is open to the scientist to abandon or qualify the theory; but she might just as well reject an auxiliary hypothesis, or question the initial conditions under which the experiment or observation was carried out. The point is that, while *something* has to be modified in the wake of the experiment, *what* is modified is not forced by the empirical facts and logic alone. Now if the choice to save or reject the theory being tested is based on pragmatic considerations alone, then the theory has not been saved or rejected on truth-related grounds. Consequently one is not entitled to believe that the theory is approximately true (if it is saved). To save or reject a scientific theory in a manner consistent with its use in answering the Big Questions one must have some truth-related grounds that allow one to weigh the credentials of (i) the recalcitrant observation(s), (ii) the initial conditions, (iii) the instruments and techniques employed, (iv) the auxiliary hypotheses, (v) the theory being tested.

Now it is generally agreed that, in practice, such judgements are guided by what have been called 'disciplinary matrices', complicated and usually implicit agreements reached by the scientific community regarding the assumptions of the discipline.[12] As we shall see in Chapter 3, many of these assumptions are of a distinctly non-empirical nature.[13] But the point for our present purposes is that, while the sociological aspects of the disciplinary matrices have been widely recognized and accepted, what has not been emphasized sufficiently is the philosophical nature of the problem, for it is simply another kind of aporia, for (i)–(v) are individually plausible but incompossible. How does one decide in a principled fashion which of (i)–(v) to abandon? Again, this is not a straightforwardly empirical question.

Several important points follow from this discussion of the insufficiency thesis. The first is that there is in fact serious business for philosophers qua philosophers to sink their teeth into even when it comes to the investigation of empirical reality, business that cannot be farmed out to the sciences. Much more will be said in Chapter 3 on the way that philosophy, metaphysics in particular, is crucial to the scientific investigation of empirical reality. But the point here is that scientific activity is a co-operative venture between the sciences and philosophy, with each having their distinctive contribution to make. This means that the redundancy thesis is false.

Secondly, the digression on the insufficiency thesis brought out the logical shape of distinctly philosophical problems. Philosophical problems are *aporetic*. We have seen that aporia arise at the level of scientific theories themselves when two or more theories appear to offer incompatible accounts of reality. They also arise when a scientist is faced with a recalcitrant observation, and the scientist faces the task of modifying something in his initial commitments that he previously found to be compelling. In both cases prima facie attractive lines of thought or commitments are found to be in tension. Something has to give. Deciding in a principled fashion what must be abandoned or qualified is the burden of philosophical reflection.

Thirdly, the aporia mentioned so far have their provenance in the sciences. But there is no reason to think that philosophical problems will be confined to technical matters of a strictly scientific nature. In fact aporia are to be found across all cognitive domains, and they extend as well into the sphere of action, both private and collective. And it is here that the relevance of philosophy to the general public at large becomes clear for all to see. The next section looks at aporia arising at the level of the social order itself. This involves examining the tensions between our commitments in the sciences, politics and economics. This takes philosophy out of the halls of academe and into the wider world.

The human predicament and the social order

I begin this section with some potted sociology. At one point in human history, before the first agricultural revolution 10,000 years ago, human beings lived in relatively small groups of closely related individuals, usually amounting to no more than 80 to 120 souls. These early societies lived very close to nature, and had a relatively simple structure with little or no division of labour. Each family had to gather its own food and water, find fibres or skins for clothing, find its own fuel for heating and cooking and find its own building materials for shelter. Securing such resources on a sustainable basis was the abiding feature of the human predicament. And it remains so to this day.

Of course very few of us today obtain our resource requirements as we did in the Palaeolithic and Neolithic periods, that is, by engaging in behaviours that put us directly in contact with the external environment. No one in the developed world grows all their own food, makes their own clothes out of fibres they themselves have gathered or grown, while also gathering or producing the necessary building materials with which to construct their own house, while also mining, drilling or foraging for wood or dung to get the materials with which to heat their house and cook their food. And the reason for this is that meeting our resource requirements is now very much a *co-operative* venture involving huge numbers of individuals, the vast majority of whom we do not know and never will know. We now live in a social order with complicated hierarchies and social differentiations. Perhaps most importantly, our social order has a division of labour that has reached a very advanced stage indeed. The upshot is that we no longer have to do everything ourselves (mercifully) because we now secure the vast majority of our material needs from the external environment *indirectly* by participating *directly* in the collective activities of the social order to which we belong, an order which touches upon the external environment only at the periphery.

Now, for good or ill, we all depend on the smooth running of the social order to which we belong. We have left the Palaeolithic phase of our history, and we have lost the skills necessary to survive without the support of the collective activities of our social order (at least in anything like our current numbers). To put it picturesquely, a complex social order is now as vital to our way of life as the dam, web and nest are to beavers, spiders and birds. The viability of one's social order is, therefore, something that matters. Of course one must guard against excessive glorification of one's social order; but we can all agree that a social order is at the very least 'a night's shelter in the wilderness'. Indeed, a cursory glance at the predicament of life in so-called 'failed states' should be enough to drive this point home. What is not so obvious is that philosophy might have something to do with the smooth running of social orders. But that is precisely what I want to consider now.

I want to suggest that there are aporetic tensions that emerge at the level of our social order. To appreciate this point we need a clear account of what a social order is, and what its collective activities are. Following the lead of sociologist Ernest Gellner, we can take the collective institutions and practices of any social order to fall into three core categories: the productive/economic, the coercive/political and the cognitive/legitimative.[14] A brief word on each is in order here. Firstly, every social order has to provide for the material needs of its members. It is these productive activities which secure raw materials from the external environment, turn these into finished goods for direct consumption and eventually distribute these amongst the members of the social order. There are various ways in which these economic activities can be organized, and each way leaves its characteristic stamp on the fabric of the social order. In addition to a productive/economic sector, every society has to have some mechanism by means of which it arrives at decisions regarding the collective activities of the social order. How are land and other resources to be divided up? How are conflicts to be resolved? How is the group to respond to natural disasters like a drought or flooding? How does the group respond to aggression from without? These sorts of issues are addressed by the politico/coercive dimension of the social order. Again there are various ways of meeting these challenges, each leaving its characteristic mark on the social order. Finally, every social order has to have a method by means of which it arrives at authoritative knowledge claims about the world in which we make our way. This is the cognitive, or knowledge-producing and legitimating, sector of the social order. Now every social order of any complexity has to find some way of carrying out these functions, and distinct social orders can be characterized by the different ways in which these functions are carried out.

But it is not enough for a social order to have the means to carry out these functions adequately. Every society needs some way of maintaining the order in its existing forms in the three domains, a 'stabilizer' so to speak. The crucial role of the stabilizer is to 'sell' its arrangements to its members. The members of a social order have to buy into the 'vision' that animates it, thereby securing their loyalty based on the feeling that the order is in some way legitimate. This task of meeting our societal needs in an acceptable manner is a challenge faced by any social order if it is to remain viable. This stabilizing function is largely a matter of socialization, a process in which the arrangements of the social order are explained and justified. This is largely a matter of becoming inculcated with, and versed in, an order's 'images of the world', to use Weber's phrase. It is these 'images' that shape how a social order goes about meeting the functions of the three domains:

> Interests (material and ideal), not ideas, dominate directly the actions of men. Yet the 'images of the world' created by these ideas have very often served as switches determining the tracks on which the dynamism of interests kept actions moving.[15]

Putting some flesh on these rather abstract bones, we can turn to the ideas behind the 'images of the world' at work in the social order of modernity:

- The West's key idea in the *cognitive/legitimative* order is the commitment to the sciences. Much has already been said about our deference to and reliance upon the sciences, and so no more need be said about it here.
- The West's central idea in the *productive/economic* order is to eschew both centrally administered economies (on the model of the Soviet Union, say) and totally unregulated exchange economies. The West has opted for mixed economies in which national governments allow markets to operate in those domains in which they work well, while providing those goods and services which even open and perfectly competitive markets cannot meet. Governments in mixed economies also provide a litany of services which enable the markets to work as well as they can. More will be said on this score shortly.
- The West's core idea in the *coercive/political* order is representative democracy combined with constitutionalism. This order is characterized by a cluster of ideas including the expectation that rulers rule with consent of the ruled;

> that consent, and therefore political legitimacy, is conferred in elections on the basis of one person, one vote; that freedom from the arbitrary will of rulers is essential; that freedom from arbitrary rule is secured by a balance and division of powers between a legislature, an executive and a judicial branch of government.

These are the core commitments of modernity. Some of these commitments are shared with other social orders, but the combination is distinctly Western.

Now the viability of any social order depends upon a healthy majority of its members feeling secure about that order's ability to meet their needs. Usually confidence in a social order's ability to deliver is maintained by that social order's track record, that is, it's actually having delivered. But confidence in its ability to continue to deliver can be shaken – natural disasters, economic shocks, wars, significant social, political and economic inequalities, civil unrest, the atomization of society, even the mere perception of one's order falling behind a competitor, all can undermine confidence in a social order. And as one commentator notes, this is not just a theoretical possibility, but very much a contemporary reality:

> Social instability became acute in Western civilization during the nineteenth century. It became permanent in the twentieth century as a result of the emancipation of the individual from the ties of tradition, especially in the form of religion, of the increased rationalisation of life and work, and of cyclical economic crises.[16]

These lines resonate today in the wake of the 2008 banking crisis, ever increasing economic inequality, looming environmental catastrophe, politically intractable humanitarian crises on the borders of Europe, the challenge to the world order posed by a resurgent Russia and an emerging China, all combined with the suspicion that the political elites of Western democracies favour the interests of pressure groups and large corporations rather than those of the people at large. Undoubtedly the West is undergoing a period of unsettling change, not to say a crisis of confidence.[17]

In such searching times the very foundations of a social order can come into question. And when this happens, the 'images of the world' that serve to legitimize the social order in the eyes of its members become the focus of attention. If these images fail to make sense of the social order, if that world view fails to be compelling, if the individuals of the social order lose confidence in these images, the social order can itself disintegrate.[18]

Now it is my view that the systematic and sustained scrutiny, maintenance, defence, as well as the overturning, of these images all require characteristically *philosophical* reflection. This is the broader social function of philosophy per se (to speak like an anthropologist). For our social order is comprised of a set of ideas and images relating to the sciences, politics and economics, each of which we in the West have found compelling in isolation, but which, as we shall see shortly, give rise to serious tensions when taken together. The need to deal with aporia such as these is why philosophy matters beyond the halls of academe, for they will not be resolved by simply doing more science.

Tensions in the social order of the West

What are these tensions? We have seen that the social order has three core component activities. The tensions that concern us now arise when the activities or commitments of one of these components undermine the activities and commitments of another. We can begin with tensions arising between the economic and political orders:

(a) Political power in the West is centred at the *national* level with the various houses of *elected representatives*. It is the nation state – as opposed to an empire, a faith or a dynastic house – that is our basic political unit. And our historical experiences of monarchies and dictatorships of all sorts (theological, communist and fascist) re-enforce the image that political power should stem from the ruled, and be wielded on behalf of the ruled. But these images sit uneasily with other features of the social order. Economic power is now *transnational*. Globalization is seemingly the natural extension of the West's commitment to trade and exchange economies in general and our rejection of centrally administered economies and protectionism. And this is not just a matter of a theoretical commitment to the ideology of comparative advantage. In 1820, 94 per cent of the world's population lived on less than $2 a day. By 2015 that figure had dropped to less than 10 per cent. International trade regimes appear to have had a lot to do with the reduction in global levels of destitution, which is clearly an important achievement. But globalization is not entirely benign. While the equality gap between nations has diminished significantly, inequalities within the domestic arena have increased dramatically. And this is because international trade inevitably brings disruptions that affect domestic income distribution. Now in the normal course of political life in democracies the electorate expects its elected officials to deal with problems arising in the social order on its behalf. But now that economic power is transnational, our elected officials have little power to control the most important forces shaping the social order. We confer political legitimacy and responsibility via elections to representatives who, through no fault of their own, lack the power to control important matters of public concern. Responsibility without power is an uncomfortable position to be in. And our choices are not obvious. Do we accept a significantly diminished national sovereignty (contra our political images), or do we retreat from the global-exchange economy (contra our economic images)? Neither is without its hazards, but a choice appears forced. This clash of images presents a classic aporia.[19]

This is not the only tension between the political and economic orders.

(b) Democracies with a near universal franchise are vulnerable to economic ruin. Governments in mixed economies are expected to provide a range of services designed to reduce transaction costs in the exchange economy while responding to domestic social demands. These services include the provision of peace and security, transportation systems, logistics, communication systems, courts (for the enforcement of contracts), a stable currency, a national bank, enforcement of rules to deal with externalities (e.g. pollution regulation), checks on the power of monopolies of any kind, basic scientific research (technological innovation), basic welfare (for those unable to work, or temporarily out of work), mass education (provision of a skilled work force), health care or the provision of health insurance (a sick labour force cannot work).

How are these vital services to be paid for? Governments in our social order have only two sources of revenue: taxation or borrowing on international money markets. Neither is straightforward. The electorate seldom consents to being taxed at rates that cover expected government spending. The expedient short-term solution (the only solution that makes sense to politicians whose sights cannot extend beyond the next election) is government borrowing and long-term debt. The only alternatives are to grow the economy in order to increase tax revenues without undue pain to the electorate, or to cut government spending. Growing the economy means engaging with globalization, which has its own difficulties. Cuts in government spending can only go so far before the electorate rebels at the polls. Most accept that bringing financial ruin upon our grandchildren by building up unsupportable levels of public debt is morally irresponsible. But limiting the franchise is unthinkable. Again we have a clash of images at the heart of our social order – the way the political order is organized appears to undermine the long-term health of our economic order, and vice versa.

If the first two tensions are politico-economic, there are others centred on the role of the sciences in our social order. The sciences are meant to provide authoritative information that feeds into the making of public policy, and, more generally, set the boundaries of rational belief and debate. But this vital role sits side by side with an unease and even suspicion of the sciences in the general public who form the electorate, an unease which can lead to defection from the sciences. More specifically,

(c) The results of the sciences are supposed to feed into the political/economic systems as the authoritative source of information. But as noted in the previous section, the sciences do not all sing from the same hymn sheet. How do we know what to believe? Now many practicing scientists, and many philosophers of science, not to mention postmodern relativists, avoid the contradictions between scientific theories by adopting an anti-realist stance towards them – that is, presenting theories not as accounts of reality that are homing in on the truth of things, but as mere instruments of prediction and control. But whatever the philosophical merits of such a stance, it is *not* compatible with the role of the sciences as the cognitive legitimizer of our social order. So the prima facie contradictions between the sciences must be worked through and removed if the authority of the sciences in the cognitive/legitimative domain is to remain intact. Until that is accomplished there will a temptation in some to defect from our commitment to the sciences.

This temptation is encouraged by a further consideration:

(d) Science tells us what is rational to believe about the natural and social orders. But it also tells us that there are no objective values. This is no small matter. Weber famously described modern Western society as 'disenchanted', and he saw this disenchantment as the root cause of the discontents our society is prey to.[20]

Weber's account of our disenchanted society begins with his observation that proper human behaviour is behaviour to which an agent attaches 'meaning'.[21] An action can be meaningful, and also rational, in two distinct ways. Firstly, an action can be meaningful and rational if it serves a purpose. Secondly, an action can be meaningful if it embodies a value. Weber also argues that human beings need to see their actions and their lives in general as part of a meaningful whole, where meaning is taken in both the instrumental and value-oriented senses. It is this need to see oneself and one's society as part of a meaningful totality that Weber identifies as the primary motivation behind religious and philosophical thought.

Now the distinguishing feature of modern Western society is that the natural sciences have taken over the role previously played by religion and philosophy. This has been a mixed blessing. On the positive side the sciences have been supremely successful in terms of increasing our technological competence and our instrumental rationality. But the downside is that the sciences are taken to militate very strongly against the idea that the universe as a whole, our society or our individual actions have any ultimate purpose or value. We are thus left in a disenchanted world, a world in which we know very well how to achieve ultimately pointless ends. The result is the increasing implementation of instrumental rationality in the social, political and economic spheres (the so-called 'iron cage' of rational administration and ever expanding bureaucracy) while we are forced to recognize that the values which fix the ends towards which instrumental rationality is directed are nothing more than subjective attitudes for which no rational justification is possible.[22] But the *legitimacy* of our political and economic systems depends upon our being able to say that they are the best of an admittedly bad lot, and that we ought to encourage the spread of these approaches not just from a self-interested point of view but for the good of those who do not as yet live under such systems. But we can't have it both ways. Either science is wrong to say that values have no grounding in fact, which would appear to compromise our image of the objectivity of the scientific enterprise, or we have to live with the idea that in politics, economics and international relations there is just brute power – no legitimacy to speak of, no right or wrong, no good or bad.

Now Weber recognizes that it is psychologically difficult to live with a world view that insists on a sharp cleavage between objective facts (as determined by the sciences) and subjective values (deemed to be a product of one's socialization). His solution, shared with Nietzsche, that *we* must *give* meaning to our lives, and strive to live by the highest values *we* find compelling, is of dubious coherence, and is unlikely to get one through the dark nights of the soul. And in these moments of stress we are likely to defect from the basic images of our world view, and be tempted to reject precisely those elements of our social order that have played a vital role in our achieving the degree of technological competence we now take for granted. Like Tolstoy, in such moments of discontent many will be tempted to say, 'Science is meaningless because it gives no answer to our question, the only question important for us: What shall we do and how shall we live?' Again, we have a tension in the basic images at the heart of our social order.

These are amongst the most pressing tensions currently in operation in our social order. And they raise precisely the sorts of questions that are not amenable to treatment by standard scientific method. Indeed, our commitment to the sciences is partly responsible for these very tensions. This is further proof of the falsity of the redundancy thesis. *Philosophical* reflection is required if these sorts of tensions are to be addressed in a rigorous and systematic fashion.

Medieval answers to modern questions

We have now reached the point where medieval philosophy, and scholasticism in particular, can be brought into the picture. Assuming for the sake of argument that we have established the need for strictly philosophical reflection to deal with pressing aporia arising in the sciences and the social order, we can ask the next obvious questions: What would such a philosophy look like? Is there a philosophy on the books capable of addressing these sorts of issues? In short, is there a philosophy that matters?

The guiding assumption of this book is that a philosophy that matters must be one which can address the sorts of aporia outlined in the previous section. This means that a philosophy that matters must be at home in the real world. A philosopher who hopes to offer the prospect of compelling resolutions to our aporia – compelling, that is, to those outside the halls of academe – must take on board and feel the attraction of the presuppositions of the sciences and the images of our social order, and then deal with the tensions to be found within them. A philosophy that fails to do this will not resonate widely beyond the lecture hall.

I submit, therefore, that a philosophy that matters must include the following: (a) an unshakable respect for common sense in order to remain 'this-worldly' and in contact with the views of the philosophical laity; (b) a faith in the methods of the sciences as our surest path to knowledge of the empirical world and (c), in the realm of value, ethics, politics and economics, the conviction that certain states of affairs are to be avoided while others are to be welcomed. Examples of objectively bad states of affairs include being forced to live in squalor surrounded by despair, destitution, disease, malnutrition, morbidity and early death; objective goods include joy, prosperity, health, security, contentment and longevity. These are amongst the basic presuppositions of the philosophical laity. Philosophers who fail to respect them do so at their peril.

Now I will be arguing that medieval philosophy matters because, unlike much contemporary philosophy, the scholastics accept (a)–(c) unequivocally. The scholastics fully respect the sciences while taking common sense as its touchstone. The scholastics provide the most sophisticated conceptual framework developed to date which is consistent with the views of the philosophical layperson while providing the metaphysical underpinnings of contemporary science. And this means that medieval philosophy can speak to contemporary concerns in surprising ways. What is more, the scholastic metaphysical framework overcomes the fact–value distinction that lies at the heart of Weberian disenchantment, thereby holding out the prospect of an objective assessment of political and economic arrangements, and the prospect of legitimacy in the realm of value. I am aware of no other philosophical framework with this collection of virtues. Odd as it sounds, medieval thinkers had answers to modern problems.[23] To rediscover the scholastics is therefore to rediscover how philosophy can be relevant, how philosophy can matter.

The rest of this book is an elaboration and defence of this thesis. The next two chapters will be devoted to exploring the deep connections between scholasticism and common sense, and between scholasticism and the sciences. Then, in Chapters 3–5, we will delve into some of the key characteristics of the medieval approach to philosophizing in general. I will end by considering a scholastic approach to Weberian disenchantment.

CHAPTER ONE

Scholasticism and common sense

This chapter begins the case for medieval philosophy by highlighting the fact that scholastic metaphysics and epistemology are quite consciously developed with an eye to saving common sense beliefs. While Thomas Reid and G. E. Moore also defend common sense, their efforts are largely confined to combating the views of other philosophers who would deny or go beyond common sense, while the scholastics focus rather on the construction of an elaborate conceptual framework which takes common sense beliefs as axiomatic. These points are illustrated by focusing on two classic problems: the problem of universals, and the problem of change. The thrust is that the scholastic solution to these problems will prove attractive to the philosophical layperson, while the alternatives will strike her as paradoxical. The scholastic solutions also provide the basis for the sciences, the topic of the next chapter.

Introduction

In the concluding section of Book I of *A Treatise of Human Nature* David Hume (1989) makes some remarkable admissions. After several pages in which he acknowledges the difficulties facing those who would venture out onto troubled philosophical seas, after admitting his own worries about falling into philosophical error and his lack of success in finding followers, after admitting that his own reflections have led him to 'the most deplorable condition imaginable, inviron'd with the deepest darkness, and utterly depriv'd of the use of every member and faculty', after all this he confesses that 'nature' cures him of his 'philosophical melancholy and delirium':

> I dine, I play a game of back-gammon, I converse, and am merry with my friends; and when after three or four hour's amusement, I wou'd return to these speculations, they appear so cold, and strain'd and ridiculous, that I cannot find in my heart to enter into them any farther. (p. 268)

Here Hume attests to the fact that the spell cast by his own philosophical reflections is broken once he gets back to the humdrum of everyday life. This passage is likely to strike a chord with many who have studied philosophy. All too often what is discussed in all seriousness in a philosophy class appears fanciful once one leaves the lecture hall. But the really curious aspect of this passage is what Hume makes of the fact that his philosophical reflections appear 'strain'd and ridiculous' after a few hours spent with friends. Rather than revisiting his sceptical conclusions with the scepticism they themselves deserve, Hume sees here a sign of the considerable powers of our passions and non-rational nature to override the paradoxical conclusions he thinks are rightly drawn by our reason. Thus a sharp cleavage opens up between how Hume thinks one proceeds qua philosopher and how one thinks qua normal person. And since Hume is one of the great names in the philosophical canon, the take-home message for students being introduced to Hume is that there is a special set of rules one is supposed to follow when doing philosophy, rules one would not dream of applying in any other truth-directed discipline.

Hume is not the only philosopher so enamoured with the niceties of a philosophical argument as to be willing to overlook the fact that its conclusion is ridiculous. But if philosophy is to matter outside of academe, if it is to be more than a clever parlour game, then we philosophers must curb our enthusiasm for the paradoxical. Too much philosophy is 'strain'd and ridiculous' once the aura of the lecture hall recedes.

But it hasn't always been this way. True, like most of the pre-Socratics, Parmenides and Heraclitus had some peculiar ideas about the fundamental structure of reality: the one denying that change ever occurs in the natural order, the other denying that anything is ever the same from one moment to the next. And while Plato did not follow either Parmenides or Heraclitus entirely, his attempt to reconcile these two thinkers led him to posit a realm of abstract entities existing 'outside' space and time, entities no one had ever previously imagined. But Plato's most famous student would have none of this. Aristotle was convinced not only that a philosopher should *start* their reflections with beliefs shared by the majority of one's contemporaries but that they should *end* there as well. That is, Aristotle maintains that a philosopher has a credible solution to a philosophical problem only if that solution is consistent with common sense. If that means abandoning a thesis defended by an illustrious philosopher, then so be it.[1] We will have occasion to consider this meta-philosophy in more detail in Chapter 4. But the point for our present purposes is that Aristotle's philosophical system draws out and develops the implicit metaphysics, epistemology and ethics of ordinary life. This means that fundamental Aristotelian principles retain their plausibility long after one has left the lecture theatre, sparing us the institutionalized schizophrenia that defenders of much pre-Aristotelian and post-Cartesian philosophy must endure.

Aristotle is not the only important philosopher to respect common sense. Thomas Reid, the uncompromising critic of his contemporary Hume, and the key figure of the Scottish School of Common Sense Philosophy, worked tirelessly to overcome the philosophical mindset and conclusions popularized by Descartes. And in the early days of the twentieth century Moore once again took up the baton in defence of the views of the philosophical layperson. He in turn inspired the ordinary language philosophers associated with the Oxford of the 1950s and 1960s. But the most sophisticated thinkers to follow Aristotle's lead were the scholastics.

There is a reason why the scholastics achieved such heights of sophistication, for there is an important difference between their intellectual tasks and those of the defenders of common sense who arrive on the scene after the advent of Descartes. Reid and Moore spend much of their time defending common sense views from the attacks of other philosophers. They turned their considerable skills to the task of diagnosing the errors in the arguments of other philosophers. Now this necessary but time-consuming defensive work was never undertaken by the scholastics because it never occurred to anyone that such a defence was needed. They took common sense beliefs for granted and then set to work on the puzzles that arise once we take these beliefs seriously from a philosophical point of view. But the advent of Descartes's 'epistemological turn', inaugurated in *Discourse on Method* and the *First Meditation*, changed the programme.[2] From now on philosophers had to offer proofs for beliefs that used to be taken for granted, hence the differences in the tasks facing the scholastics and a Reid or a Moore, who find themselves on the other side of the Cartesian historical divide. While the efforts of Reid and Moore are largely confined to combating the views of other philosophers who would deny or go beyond common sense, thereby arguing *to* common sense beliefs, the scholastics were free to focus on the positive task of constructing an elaborate conceptual framework which takes common sense beliefs as axiomatic; that is, they argued *from* common sense beliefs towards a metaphysical account of what is implicit in everyday life. A result was that the best minds of Europe worked collaboratively on a common, overarching philosophical project, within a largely shared philosophical framework, over the course of several centuries. There has been nothing like it since. The level of professionalism and sophistication achieved was extraordinary. And their basic framework, the main topic of this book, continually surprises by its ability to withstand scrutiny in the light of our considerable advances in the sciences.[3]

These points are illustrated in this chapter by focusing on two classic problems: the problem of universals, and the problem of change. The moral of the story is that the scholastic solution to these problems will prove attractive to the philosophical layperson, while the alternatives will strike them as paradoxical. So if we are keen to find a philosophical voice that might get some traction outside of academe, then the scholastics have something to offer.

But first, it would be wise to pause for a moment to clarify what is meant by the terms 'common sense' and 'common sense belief'.

What counts as a common sense belief?

The term 'common sense' as employed here is something of a term of 'art'.[4] Having a common sense belief is *not* about having 'street smarts', for example, or having a general ability to deal with a tricky set of circumstances without proper preparation or warning, although in a looser, more colloquial sense this way of speaking is perfectly acceptable. Common sense beliefs in the sense which I use the term here, and in which Reid understood the term, are the fundamental elements, principles or cornerstones of the conceptual scheme lying behind the views and actions of the ordinary person. More precisely, common sense beliefs are those views regarding the nature of things which are *presupposed* by ordinary everyday beliefs and abilities. It is these 'principles of common sense', as Reid calls them, that 'massive central core of human thinking which has no history', as Strawson has it,[5] which are the common sense philosopher's main concern. Now these principles might never be explicitly entertained by the ordinary person, not because common sense beliefs are obscure, difficult or arcane but because they are so obvious that they ordinarily pass entirely unnoticed. Nevertheless, these principles must be true if the sorts of things we commonly and consciously accept as true are true.

Some examples will help fix ideas. The following are taken from Moore's first lecture in *Some Main Problems of Philosophy*. Moore claims that common sense would have it that

1. There are in the universe an enormous number of material objects (e.g. our bodies, other people, animals, plants, stones, mountains, rivers, seas, planets, tables, chairs).
2. Human beings have minds inasmuch as we have a variety of mental states, including acts of consciousness. We see, hear, feel, remember, imagine, think, believe, desire, dislike, will, love and so forth.
3. All material objects are located in space inasmuch as they are located at a distance from each other.
4. Mental acts are attached to – contained within – certain kinds of bodies (human bodies and perhaps those of the higher animals).

5. Mental acts are ontologically dependent upon bodies.
6. Most material objects have no acts of consciousness attached to them.
7. Material objects can and do exist when we are not conscious of them.
8. There was a time when no act of consciousness was attached to any material body.
9. All objects and acts of consciousness are in time.
10. We *know* (1)–(9) to be true.

Now the principal contention of common sense philosophy is that any philosophical argument, thesis or system which is inconsistent with any of this set of beliefs is almost certainly wrong, and so no lasting philosophical achievement is to be expected if these beliefs are not accommodated. But the main point for our present purposes is that the scholastics – despite their historical distance, and despite their forbidding technical language – embrace (1)–(10), and so they speak fundamentally the same language and inhabit fundamentally the same metaphysical world as today's philosophical layperson. This important point is best seen by considering two of philosophy's deepest metaphysical problems, the problem of universals and the problem of change.

The problem of universals

No period in history saw a more sustained attack on the problem of universals than the Middle Ages. For some it is the quintessential issue of the period. Although the problem fell out of fashion in the early modern period, it has regained prominence amongst metaphysicians of the twentieth-century analytic tradition. Curiously there is nothing particularly 'medieval' about the problem since it does not presuppose any distinctly theological considerations, and it had been extensively discussed by the ancient Greeks. In fact the problem arises for anyone who would try to understand the relationship between thought and extra-mental reality. The problem, which takes the form of an aporia, emerges whenever one finds a commitment to the following plausible but apparently incompatible propositions:

11 Explanatory knowledge of the natural order is possible.
12 Such knowledge is expressed in statements containing general terms and not just names of singulars.
13 A necessary condition of knowing that *p* is that *p* is true.
14 Truth is correspondence.
15 Reality contains only singulars.

These propositions need some unpacking before the problem becomes perfectly clear. One has *explanatory knowledge* of *p* when one knows not just *that p* is the case, but *why p* is the case. And one knows why *p* is the case when one knows the causes that brought about *p*. Proposition (11) says that knowledge of this type is possible regarding the natural or real order. The 'natural order' is the term used by the scholastics for what we would now refer to as the domain of the natural sciences. The natural order is that system of entities whose existence and nature is independent of what humans happen to think about it. That is, such entities can and do exist even when we humans are not conscious of them, as Moore's seventh proposition has it. The items listed in the chemist's table of elements, for instance, existed long before humans identified them, and their properties are there to be discovered, not invented, by us.[6] Now because our social order has signed up to science being the source of explanatory knowledge of how the world works, we are collectively committed to Proposition (11).

Proposition (12) says that explanatory knowledge claims are impossible to formulate without employing general terms or terms for 'natural kinds'. Some examples will help. 'Bill' and 'Betty' are proper names for singulars. Assume they are names for particular, concrete, discreet human beings. Proper names like 'Bill' and 'Betty' are different in kind from general terms like '*Homo sapiens*'. '*Homo sapiens*' is the name of a natural kind of which Bill and Betty are only two of many instances. '*Homo sapiens*' is called a general term because it can be applied to all human beings, not just to Bill or Betty, Paul or Patty. Now the important point for us is that explanatory knowledge trades in natural kind terms. (In fact all thought about the natural order, scientific or otherwise, trades in such terms.) For example, if I want to know *why* this particular piece of metal has rusted, I will advert to different kinds of elements and their interactions, iron and oxygen, say, both of which are natural kinds. I will say that this piece of metal has rusted because the metal is of a certain kind, iron, and whenever iron is brought into contact with a gas of a certain kind, oxygen, a result of a certain kind, iron oxide, is produced. Of course there is more to be said about these particular kinds and why they have these characteristic interactions, but the point is that the explanation employs terms for natural kinds. Scientific theories abound in natural kind terms: 'electron', 'proton', 'gene', 'DNA', 'cell', 'proteins' are only a few examples. By contrast, 'Bill' and 'Betty' and other proper names do not appear in scientific explanations, nor do any other terms for singulars.

Proposition (13) states a truism about knowledge. You can strongly believe what is false; you can even rationally and justifiably believe what is false, but you cannot know that *p* if *p* is false. 'Knowledge' is a success term, and the success in question here is the matter of 'getting it right'. I cannot know, for example, that gold dissolves in water, because gold does not dissolve in water. And it does not matter how many people hold a particular belief. If many millions thought that gold dissolves in water it would still not constitute knowledge. Mere belief, even widely held belief, is not knowledge.[7]

Proposition (14) is a claim about the nature of truth. The common sense view is that a belief about the natural order is true if it accurately reports on the state of affairs it purports to be about. For example, we are inclined to say that the statement 'Grass is green' is true if and only if grass is in fact green. As Aristotle puts it, 'To say of what is that it is, and to say of what is not that it is not, that is to speak the truth.' Notice that truth and knowledge are not the same thing. A belief might be true because it corresponds to the facts without anyone being in a position to know that the belief corresponds to the facts. For example, a detective's suspicions about the guilt or innocence of a suspect are often true despite the fact that there is no proof that would stand up in court.

Finally, Proposition (15) says that, at bottom, the natural order contains only singulars. If I go out into the world I won't encounter *Homo sapiens*, but I will run into Bill and Betty, Paul and Patty.

Everything that exists in the natural order is a singular thing, a mixture (e.g. blood) or an aggregate of singular things (e.g. a football team). The point here is that there are no general things to be found anywhere in existence.

Now the tension between these propositions can be laid out in relatively short order once they have been explained. How can our alleged knowledge claims be true, that is, correspond to reality, if these claims contain general terms while the world they purport to be about contains only singulars? Our thoughts are full of generalities, but the world contains no generalities. So how can our thoughts accurately represent the world? This is the problem of universals, for a 'universal' is simply another name for a general term.

Any solutions?

Let us assume for the sake of argument that no philosopher worth her salt is simply going to accept that she has inconsistent beliefs. Philosophers are supposed to have petty minds that worry about things like contradictions. So what is a philosopher to do in the face of the problem of universals?

The easiest and most direct way out of an aporia is to reject one or more of the propositions that led to trouble in the first place. So some will bite the bullet and reject the eleventh proposition. They will say, contra (11), that knowledge of the natural order (via science or any other means) is *not* possible. Those who take this route out of the dilemma are forced to embrace a form of scepticism or perhaps some form of anti-realism in the sciences (which maintains that scientific theories are only in the business of allowing for predication and control of phenomena, or the mathematical representation of a set of experimental laws). Now there is no doubt that adopting such a stance removes the dilemma, because the remaining four propositions do not in themselves lead to a contradiction. But the cost of this stance is considerable. Indeed it entails removing one of the central planks of our social order, namely the commitment to the sciences. Worse, it says there is no hope of replacing the sciences with anything better, for the problem is not with the sciences per se but with the fact that reality is not knowable by creatures such as ourselves. How, then, are we to think responsibly about the world in which we make our way, and how are we to make responsible recommendations regarding our collective actions? It is not clear that a sceptic has anything to offer on either score.

Another possibility is to deny Proposition (12), and try to show that knowledge claims can be paraphrased in such a way as to remove all instances of general terms. This would involve developing a language that had a different proper name for each and every singular object while still allowing us to think in an organized fashion about the natural order. If this were possible then again we would have a way out of the dilemma, for the remaining propositions do not lead to a contradiction. The problem is that no one has been able to construct such a language. And the reason for this failure is that the very way we humans organize the blooming and buzzing confusion of the natural order is by categorizing singular entities into distinct kinds. This is what allows us to recognize patterns and law-like regularities in the natural order, which give us a sense that we are getting to grips with what is going on around us. To give up on general terms and the concepts they express is in effect to give up on knowledge altogether as effectively as the blunt denial of Proposition (11).

Could we simply deny that knowledge requires truth? In popular culture it is in fact quite common to find people talking as though 'knowledge' is really just what everybody accepts. But as long as one wants to be able to distinguish between what passes for knowledge and the real thing, it would seem that one cannot really remove truth from the concept of knowledge. And surely we want to be able to make such a distinction. The fact that everybody happens to believe a proposition should not be enough to say that the proposition counts as knowledge. Contemporary accounts of the Black Death, for example, put it down to mysterious airborne entities.[8] The latest thinking on this is that the Black Death was caused by a bubonic parasite combined with anthrax. Now whether this latest theory is right or not, surely we don't want to say that people in the Middle Ages *knew* the cause of the plague because there were widely held views on the matter. The tragedy is in part precisely that medieval Europeans did *not* know what was causing the plague. In any case, there are very few takers for this approach to the dilemma.

Perhaps we could drop the correspondence theory of truth for propositions about the natural order? After all, there are all sorts of alternative theories of truth currently on the market.

The problem is that all of these alternative theories, while plausible in certain contexts, really fail to convince when we are dealing with propositions about the natural order. What is more obvious, truistic and banal than the claim that 'Grass is green' is true if and only if grass is green? What could lead me to say in all seriousness that 'Grass is green' is true if and only if this proposition fits with my other botanic beliefs (as coherentists would have it), or that it is true if and only if my actions based on this belief tend to go well (as pragmatists would have it), or that it is true if and only if when the science of botany is complete we find that all botanists agree that grass is green (as Pearcean pragmaticists would have it), or that 'Grass is green' is true if and only if I have a warrant to assert that grass is green (as the semantic anti-realists would have it)? Truth is a tricky concept, no doubt. But if we cannot hang on to truisms about our concepts we have little hope of making progress on more challenging topics.

Perhaps, like Plato, we could deny Proposition (15) and claim that while the natural order might contain only singulars, there is more to reality than the natural order and what supervenes upon it. Perhaps we should consider the possibility that reality contains abstract objects as well, objects that exist in some sense outside of space and time, in a realm where entities do not have to be singular, concrete and discrete. Perhaps general terms refer directly to these abstract objects, and only indirectly to concrete singulars that we find in ordinary experience. Now Plato is no philosophical lightweight, and so such a proposal deserves our attention. But it does raise a good number of difficulties, many of which were pointed out by his pupil Aristotle. Perhaps the most telling is that the positing of abstract objects leads to real epistemological difficulties. How could creatures such as ourselves ever come to know anything about such objects? What we think we know we think we can trace back to sense experience, says Aristotle. But there is no possible sense experience of abstract objects. So even if there were abstract objects, it is not obvious how this would help us out of our dilemma. If I can know the natural order only in virtue of knowing abstract objects, but I am not able to know abstract objects, then we foreclose on my having any knowledge of the natural order, and we are back to denying Proposition (11).[9]

Now there is one thing all these approaches to the problem of universals have in common. Either they all involve dropping a belief that is implicit in common sense views of the world (rejecting Propositions (11), (12), (13) and (14)) or they demand that we postulate in all seriousness entities that common sense would never dream of and which give rise to further philosophical puzzles (rejecting Proposition (15)). These are significant philosophical costs to incur in order to resolve the dilemma. Ideally we would like to find some way out of our difficulties which would allow us to retain *all* of these propositions while removing the tension between them. This would give us the benefit of no longer struggling with inconsistent beliefs without incurring the cost of violating common sense.

This is where Aristotle comes in. Aristotle and the scholastics insist on retaining all five propositions of this dilemma, and so they accept the burden of resolving the tensions between them. The first step is to admit that something is amiss with our ordinary beliefs as manifested in Propositions (11)–(15) because the contradiction looks to be genuine and not merely prima facie. But keeping faith with common sense Aristotle assumes that we must be missing something. The task, as he sees it, is to 're-imagine' reality and human minds in an effort to find some way of saving Propositions (11)–(15) without saying anything that contravenes common sense. What must reality be like for Propositions (11)–(15) to be true simultaneously? That is the question. And his answer is to introduce a distinction in the make-up of the singular things to be found within the natural order. This distinction is the basis of his famous *hylomorphism*.

The term 'hylomorphism' stems from the Greek 'hyle', meaning 'matter', and 'morphe', meaning 'shape' or 'form'. The idea is that each singular thing to be met with in the natural order – each horse, each oak tree, each carbon atom – is a composite entity made up of both matter and form. Without getting into the details here, one can think of matter as the material stuff things are composed of, and form as a pattern according to which matter can be organized. To illustrate using an example that is not to be found in Aristotle, consider the chemist's table of elements. Everything listed in this table is made up of electrons, protons and neutrons. What differentiates oxygen from carbon, say, is not what these elements are made of, for both are made up of electrons, protons and neutrons. What distinguishes oxygen from carbon is the *number* of electrons, protons and neutrons it takes to make an atom of oxygen and of carbon, and the *configuration* of the electrons, protons and neutrons. For purposes of illustration, think of the electrons, protons and neutrons as analogous to Aristotle's matter which can enter into different configurations, while the different configurations are themselves analogous to Aristotle's form. So if I want to know what carbon is I can say in good Aristotelian fashion that carbon is that element the atoms of which have six electrons, six protons and six neutrons (the matter) arranged in a particular pattern (the form). Oxygen is that element the atoms of which have eight electrons, eight protons and eight neutrons (the matter) arranged in a particular pattern (the form). Aristotle's point is that a singular carbon atom, say, is really a composite of two things: matter and form. And the same goes for all entities in the natural order. The matter of a human being and the matter of a horse is the same as the matter of carbon and oxygen, for the bodies of animals are made up of elements, and these elements are again composed of electrons, protons and neutrons. But what distinguishes a human being from a horse is the manner in which our matter is arranged, that is, our form. In biological entities the way matter is arranged is determined by each species' distinct developmental programme. Horses have a distinct development programme, as do human beings, as do cabbages, as do flies. And this is why matter that is essentially the same can be used to generate very different singular entities indeed. Developmental programmes in biological entities are Aristotelian forms.[10]

How does this help with the problem of universals? The idea is that the singular entities we find in the natural order really are singular, because each singular thing has its own 'parcel' of matter out of which it is composed, a parcel not shared with any other singular thing. So Proposition (15) is not under threat. But there is more to singular things than their matter. As we saw, matter comes arranged in a particular pattern, and patterns, unlike matter, are *shareable*. I can have two distinct lumps of matter, and so have two distinct singular things, but if these lumps of matter are arranged according to the same pattern, then, although remaining distinct, they share something significant in common. Their shared form is what makes them instances of the same natural kind. Aristotle's solution to the problem of universals is thus predicated on the view that the natural order contains only singulars, but these singulars come in natural kinds determined by their forms.

Our general concepts, so crucial to the formulation of knowledge claims regarding the natural order, refer to the shared forms of singulars. That is how our claims about singulars, although they contain general terms, can be adequate representations of states of affairs in the world.

So the standard scholastic solution to the problem of universals requires positing (i) *immanent* substantial forms in things themselves,[11] and (ii) an account of how human beings are able to generate, or otherwise acquire, general concepts that are adequate to entities that are metaphysically singular. After much debate the scholastics converged on the view that universals in the strict sense are *concepts* with a foundation in reality.[12] Each concept is itself a singular entity (an accident of a particular mind) but in virtue of being predicable of many it is called a universal. Concepts are generated via abstraction from our experience of singulars. Singulars have a tendency to induce human minds to generate concepts applicable to many singulars in virtue of the real resemblances to be found amongst them, resemblances grounded on their shared form. These concepts are arrived at by a process of selectively ignoring the individuating features of singulars while focusing on their shared characteristics.[13] But while the natural order is always richer than our conceptual representations of it, nonetheless our concepts can be adequate to real singulars because simplification is not falsification, and because at least some of these noticed resemblances are grounded in objective features of things in themselves, namely, their individual substantial form. In non-scholastic jargon, this means accepting that singulars can be adequately conceptualized as belonging to repeatable kinds or natures.

Now this minimal statement of moderate realism regarding universals is one that all the principle scholastic figures, from Aquinas to Ockham to Suarez, can accept.[14] It also allows one to respect Propositions (11)–(15), so it should be attractive to those who maintain that some account of the relationship between thought and reality that allows for the possibility of knowledge is required. And this is clearly required for those who hope to take the first-order sciences seriously, for all the sciences presuppose such an account. So in the absence of an alternative account of the relationship between thought and reality, there is pressure to embrace the notion of a nature and its correlate, substantial form. Now my suggestion is that this solution to the problem of universals should be taken seriously precisely because it solves a problem in a way that is congenial to our concern to keep contact with the beliefs of the philosophical layperson. This means countenancing the notion of 'forms' and the accompanying conceptual framework.

The problem of change

Our second problem also takes the form of an aporia whose initial premises are all implicit in ordinary common sense beliefs. Consider the following set of propositions:

16 The universe contains, amongst other things, mind-independent middle-sized items like stones, plants, animals and so forth.

17 These items can persist through some changes, but not all.

18 These items are intelligible.

Again it will not be at all obvious why this set of propositions has proved so problematic. Proposition (16) is simply a restatement of Moore's first claim. The first clarification needed is what is meant by 'middle-sized objects'. This term is used to characterize those objects that exist in the middle of a scale that begins with objects at the 'micro' level, that is, the level of the very, very small (electrons, protons and neutrons being good examples) and those at the 'macro' level, that is, stupendously large objects like galaxies. Middle-sized objects are the objects we are familiar with in ordinary life because they are easily observable by creatures of our size and sense modalities; secondly, we need to know what 'mind-independence' amounts to, but this has already been mooted in our previous discussion of the difference between the natural and social orders. Stones, plants, animals and stars are naturally occurring entities whose existence is not dependent upon what we happen to think about them. Unlike constellations, which are arbitrary groupings of stars by human observers, stars themselves are thoroughly mind independent, as are stones, plants and animals. As Moore says, these objects can and do exist when we are not conscious of them.

Proposition (17) says that mind-independent middle-sized objects are subject to change. I am such an object, and over the years I've been through some changes. Indeed I have been prey to the sorts of changes all flesh is heir to – certain measurements of interest to my tailor have altered, my health has waxed and waned, my patience for substandard political commentary has diminished and so forth. But even though I'm much crankier now than in previous years I remain fundamentally the same thing I was prior to the changes. I am still a human being despite the changes I've undergone. But there are some changes I could not suffer while remaining fundamentally the same thing. I cannot transmogrify into a stop sign and still be a human being. Such a change is incompatible with my continuing my career as a human being. And this pattern of change-within-certain-boundaries goes for all mind-independent middle-sized objects. Such objects can undergo certain changes while remaining the same thing, but some changes mark the termination of a career.

The key term in Proposition (18) is 'intelligible'. It is a shorthand way of saying that explanatory knowledge of changing middle-sized objects is possible at least in principle. If a banana is green on Monday, yellow by Thursday and brown by Sunday we think that such changes can be explained by suitably versed botanists, explanations that will be able to show why the banana went from being green to being brown, and not from green to blue (say). Similar explanations are available for the changes I have gone through as well.

Now even with this unpacking it is unlikely that the problem of change will be fully apparent. But ever since Parmenides metaphysicians have been troubled by the idea that real entities can persist through change. Perhaps the easiest way to see the difficulty is as follows: if one assumes that an item, a banana, say, has persisted through a change, then we have committed ourselves to saying that the banana prior to the change is the same item as the banana at the end of the process (the banana when green and the banana when brown are the same banana). But according to Leibniz's law (and, it would appear, common sense) if one thing is numerically identical to another thing, then any property of the one must also be a property of the other. But if our banana has undergone a change then it must have some property after the change that it previously did not have, or must have lost a property it previously had. In either case the banana when green does *not* have the same properties as the banana when brown; so by Leibniz's law the banana at the start cannot be the banana we have at the end, and so the banana has *not* persisted through the change but has been replaced by a numerically distinct banana. Generalize this result and one ends up denying that change is possible.

Now, as with the problem of universals, philosophers have tended to solve this aporia by denying one of Propositions (16)–(18). But again, denying any of these propositions puts a metaphysician seriously at odds with the views of the ordinary philosophical layperson, for they all amount to denying that change as normally understood is in fact possible in real things. They might, like Parmenides, insist that change is an illusion. Change might appear to be happening in the real world, he says, but it isn't really. This is tantamount to denying (16), because it is denying what we are aware of through sense experience is real, and what we are aware of is changing middle-sized objects. Another familiar option, popular amongst some physicists and some metaphysicians, is to admit that sense experience puts us in touch with a world that appears to be changing (so sense experience is not deceiving us) but to deny that middle-sized and macro-sized objects are in fact *fully* real. This line of thought would have it that a banana, say, is not fully real because bananas are merely accidental aggregations of atoms. And the basis of this discrimination is change itself. The idea is that atoms themselves do not undergo change, and this is what makes them fully real, while aggregations come and go, giving the appearance of change. But since Parmenides has shown that change is impossible, we must assume that it isn't happening in real things; *ergo* aggregates are not real things. The fact that common sense would have it that stones, plants, animals, stars and the like are as 'real' as anything can be and certainly as real as their component parts is neither here nor there on this approach.

Another option is to advert to the notions of perdurance and temporal parts. On this line one offers a radical reinterpretation of objects and nature of change. Contrary to common sense, only a part of an object exists at any one moment. It is not the case that an object endures by being wholly present at every moment it exists. Now setting aside the fact that such theories really amount to the denial that change occurs,[15] and setting aside questions regarding the internal coherence of perdurance theories,[16] those inclined to take common sense seriously might think, 'So much the worse for those who deny the reality of middle-sized objects and change as a real feature of the living world. We ought to have more confidence in common sense than the reflections of metaphysicians.'[17] But there is one metaphysical theory that quite deliberately makes room for the endurance theory of change, namely, Aristotelian essentialism.

Aristotelian essentialism

Aristotle's essentialism, the basic outlines of which are accepted by the scholastics, is the result of the attempt to provide a metaphysical account of what is implicit in our everyday dealings with the world. In particular the essentialist wants to maintain Propositions (16)–(18). As noted above, the problem posed by this set of propositions has been to understand how real items can persist through change. Aristotle's solution is to accept the following claims:[18]

19 The world is primarily constituted by singulars belonging to discrete natural kinds.

20 Each kind has a set of essential properties.

21 A property is an essential feature of a kind if and only if it is a feature used to define the kind.

22 The definition of a kind plays two important roles. Firstly, the definition provides the existence and identity conditions of instances of the kind. These allow one to track an instance of a kind through its career and any changes it might undergo by allowing principled answers to questions of the form 'is *a* the same as *b*?' Secondly, a definition stating the essence of a kind has an explanatory role in that it is adverted to when explaining why an instance of the kind has the properties and behaviour patterns that it does.

23 Propositions (19)–(22) are grounded in the nature of things independently of our thought or representations of them.

Such a theory allows the essentialist to maintain the target theses at the expense of some qualification of Leibniz's law (it does not apply unqualifiedly across times). Propositions (19) and (23) do justice to the reality of middle-sized items; propositions (20), (21) and the first part of (22) accommodate the claim that these items can persist through some changes but not all by distinguishing between essential and non-essential properties; the loss of the latter is consistent with the continued existence of the items through the change, while the loss of the former marks the passing out of existence of the item in question; Proposition (21) and the second part of (22) mark a commitment to the intelligibility of these items. Crucial to the position is the distinction between essential and non-essential properties, a distinction based on the previously drawn distinction between a singular's matter and form. Only if such a distinction is recognized can an entity undergo a change without passing out of existence altogether: accommodating this common sense view is the primary motivation behind essentialism.

Providing a metaphysics which allows one to uphold (16)–(18) is difficult without recourse to essentialism; indeed every competing metaphysical system abandons one or more of the target theses. For example, in asserting the mind-independent nature of middle-sized items the essentialist is at odds with Kant and all forms of constructivism. The essentialist's commitment to (16) distinguishes him from Plato (who maintained, at one stage at least, that extra-temporal and spatial forms alone are ultimately real), from Democritus and other atomists (who reduced middle-sized, and all composite, items to aggregates of atoms, the latter alone being fully real) and from Spinoza (who maintained that there is only *one* ontologically basic item). Proposition (17) distinguishes the essentialist from Heraclitus, modern-day phenomenalists, and trope theorists (who deny the existence of *persisting* objects of any kind). The essentialist's commitment to (16) and (17) together distinguishes him from Parmenides, Plato, Heraclitus, Democritus and modern-day perdurance theorists who deny that any change is possible in real entities, and from Spinoza who maintains that all changes are merely phase changes of one underlying substance. Finally the essentialist's commitment to (18) distinguishes him from Parmenides, Heraclitus, Plato and the skeptics and scientific anti-realists who all denied that the world of ordinary sense experience is intelligible.

So the first point to drive home here is that the rejection of essentialism comes at a high price to ordinary common sense intuitions. If one is inclined to believe that individual horses and cabbages, say, are as real as anything can be, that an individual horse and individual cabbage can undergo some changes while remaining a horse or a cabbage respectively, while other changes bring about their respective ends, and if one believes that we can understand something of horses and cabbages (e.g. that we can explain why horses have the standard vertebrate limb and cabbage plants can photosynthesize), then Aristotle's essentialism proves indispensable, for the other major metaphysical systems threaten precisely these sorts of claims.[19] A second, broader, point follows immediately upon the first, namely, that a philosophy with a chance of mattering outside the halls of academe must cleave to essentialism, for losing touch with the views of the philosophical laity is the fast track to irrelevance. If philosophers need to find a language in which to speak to those outside academe, they should learn to speak Aristotelian.

But keeping in touch with common sense is only one of the features of a philosophy that matters. As I suggested at the end of Chapter 1, a philosophy that matters must also be in a position to take the sciences seriously. That is, a philosopher who wishes to be able to speak to the aporia outlined in Chapter 1 must be willing to accept that mature scientific theories are not merely instruments of prediction and control, but are truth-apt representations of reality. For if one does not accept that the sciences are in the business of informing us on the workings of the natural order, then one has no business adverting to the sciences when considering public policy.

Now what we have seen in this chapter is that scholastic Aristotelian principles are precisely what are needed to preserve the intelligibility of the natural order. Firstly, it is only if our general terms and concepts are adequate to things that our thoughts and statements themselves can be adequate to things. And as we saw, the scholastic solution to the problem of universals is the smoothest way of securing this result. Similarly, if we cannot be confident that the ordinary objects of sense experience are as real as anything can be despite the changes they undergo, how are we to come to know anything else? Of course there is more to the natural order than the middle-sized objects of everyday life. But we think that we come to know about these additional features of reality by inferring their existence and nature from what we are able to observe. If what we can observe is not real, what can we safely infer from these 'illusory' data? Thus it would appear that the scholastic solution to the problem of change is also a precondition of the viability of science. Indeed, these scholastic positions on the problem of universals and the problem of change are the bedrock of the sciences, a topic to be continued in the next chapter.

CHAPTER TWO

Scholasticism and the sciences

Many still labour under the false impression that medieval thought was inimical to the sciences, and that the sciences did not begin to flourish until scholasticism was overthrown. This view has now been so thoroughly discredited by historians that little time need be spent on it here. What is less commonly discussed is how thoroughly imbued with metaphysical commitments the natural sciences are, and that these commitments are precisely those of the scholastics and decidedly not those of empiricism or any other school. The preceding chapter's discussion of the problem of universals and the problem of change provided two cases in point. This chapter goes on to show how the methodology of the sciences, particularly the design of experiments, also presupposes scholastic principles. This is doubly important: firstly, the connection between scholasticism and the sciences is further established at a very deep level indeed; secondly, given that the general public is constantly bombarded with the latest scientific experimental results on virtually every aspect of modern life, a vital connection between scholasticism and everyday experience is also established. If scientific experiments matter, then so does medieval philosophy.

Introduction

In the previous chapter an attempt was made to illustrate the fundamental point that scholastic metaphysical principles are consistent with the views of the ordinary philosophical layperson. This is important because a precondition of philosophy interacting meaningfully with those outside academe is a broadly shared framework of ideas. Commitment to Reid's principles of common sense provides that shared framework: the scholastics and the man on the street live in much the same world, and so are in a good position to understand what the other is saying about that world. Rejecting that framework makes mutual comprehension, and so meaningful engagement, that much harder to achieve.

But no one – not even common sense philosophers, and certainly not the scholastics – thinks that a complete inventory of common sense principles will exhaust or even begin to exhaust all there is to know about the natural order. Common sense principles give us only the bare outlines of an account of reality. True, these outlines are fundamental to that account, but they are only outlines. The flesh on the bones of the common sense view of the world is to be provided by the careful empirical investigation of the natural order. This means the first-order disciplines, in particular the sciences, have an indispensable part to play in the co-operative effort of making sense of the world we live in. But this respect for the sciences is in no way inimical to common sense, or to the scholastics. On the contrary, the sciences are deeply committed to scholastic principles. In the previous chapter we saw that an answer to the problem of universals is necessary if the sciences are to be possible at all. Similarly, an answer to the problem of change is necessary if a science of the middle-sized objects of chemistry, biology, geology, psychology and the social sciences is to be possible. Now I suggested that it is the scholastics who provide the smoothest handling of these issues, while other metaphysical systems struggle with precisely these preconditions of the sciences. In this chapter I go further and look at the presuppositions of scientific method to re-enforce just how deep the commitment of the sciences is to scholastic metaphysical principles.

But two preliminary points are worth dwelling on for a moment. Firstly, a very quick glance at the historical work that has already been done to establish that the sciences are best seen as a development, not as an abandonment of scholastic principles, is necessary, for this prejudice remains firmly entrenched in the contemporary mind despite the decades of research that have established precisely the opposite. Secondly, there is a view amongst academics and the general public that the sciences do not rely on metaphysical principles of any description, let alone those of the scholastics. The sciences, the positivists told us, represent a world historical moment when the modes of thought typical of philosophers, particularly 'armchair' metaphysical speculation, were abandoned in favour of the experimental rigour of scientific method. Now in Chapter 1 we saw that this picture is *not* sustainable. But it is worth reminding ourselves of this point before going on to consider just how much metaphysics is needed to get the empirical investigation of the natural order off the ground. These points covered, we can then move on to show that the metaphysics needed to achieve this is that of the scholastics.

Medieval thought and the emergence of the modern sciences

> One of the strands of the historical narrative with which we are concerned is the progress which is made on occasion through the development of scholastic thinking itself. In other words, the modern world is in a certain sense a continuation of the medieval one – it is not to be regarded as merely a reaction against it. As a result of this some historians of science have been disposed seriously to qualify the traditional concept of the 'Renaissance', and to see, from the eleventh and twelfth century at least, a continuous development of western thought.
>
> BUTTERFIELD, 1957, pp. 15–16

> One of the most surprisingly successful bluffs in the history of philosophy ... has caused empiricism to be taken to be specially apt for the explanation of science
>
> MARTIN, 1988, p. 72

Pierre Duhem's groundbreaking work on the history of science opened the floodgates to countless studies on medieval science and the transition to early modernity.[1] His central thesis, that modern science begins with events deep in the thirteenth century, set the agenda for subsequent historians of science, receiving both strong support and critical attention. Duhem's thesis attracted so much comment in the early days because it ran counter to the then-prevailing view that early modernity was primarily a reaction against, not a continuation of, medieval modes of thought. This widespread assumption was not wholly unfounded. The transition in cosmology from the Ptolemaic to the Copernican systems required significant modifications to Aristotelian physics. And there was, of course, the infamous case of Galileo to underwrite the allegation that the Church is inherently hostile to the sciences. But what Duhem and subsequent historians have found is that the transition from the Middle Ages to early modernity is marked as much by continuity as by innovation. Indeed some historians, following le Goff, have taken to talking about the 'long Middle Ages', suggesting that the Middle Ages did not end conveniently in 1500, but continued well into the seventeenth and even eighteenth centuries.[2]

The continuity thesis begins to make sense when one leaves aside the details of particular scientific theories and one focuses instead on the background assumptions that must be in place for scientific study of the natural order to make sense.[3] These assumptions come to the fore when one considers the historical origins of the scientific world view. Historians of science have been keen to determine why it is the sciences as we know them arose in Western Europe as opposed to anywhere else. This is a bit of a puzzle because at the time of the scientific revolution Western Europe was not a world leader in any obvious respect. Other peoples at the time were far more sophisticated and refined than the rough, smelly and rather barbarous populations of Europe. So why did the scientific project, a world historic event, emerge in this relative backwater? Another way to put the question is to ask why the sciences as we know them did *not* arise amongst the Ottomans, the Safavids in Persia, the Mughal Empire in India, or in the China of the Ming or the Qing. Was the scientific revolution some kind of accident, or did medieval Europe lay the groundwork for the emergence of the sciences?

Much work remains to be done in this field, but the results so far suggest that the emergence of the sciences in Europe was no accident. On the contrary, it would appear that medieval thought – an uneasy synthesis of Greek philosophy, Roman law, Jewish religious thought and the Christian New Testament – is the soil out of which science develops. This makes medieval thought a precondition of, rather than an impediment to, the emergence of empirical studies of the natural order. This 'soil' is a collection of assumptions about the natural order that need to be in place before serious study of it is likely to be undertaken, assumptions not necessarily shared by the more sophisticated and refined contemporaries of medieval Europe.

The first necessary assumption is that the natural order is in fact an *order* and not a haphazard collection of entities and events. There can be no systematic study of disconnected facts or pieces of information. Only an ordered cosmos is in principle intelligible because intelligibility depends on the fact that the components of an order all 'hang together' in systematic relations. Tracking these relations is what constitutes understanding. Now one of the key claims of the Hebraic religions is that the created world is the handiwork of a *rational* God. It is, therefore, intelligible, at least in principle. The intelligibility of the natural order is emphasized by the scholastics time and time again in the claim that 'God does nothing in vain'. Things don't just happen willy-nilly in the natural order. Everything that happens happens for a reason. The *Principe of Sufficient Reason*, so loved of philosophers, has its ultimate justification in the assumption of a rational creator.[4]

A second assumption about the natural order is necessary before it can be studied systematically in the manner of the modern sciences. It has to be *de-animated*. If the natural order were really an extended *social* order, then we would be debarred from approaching it in the manner of the experimental sciences. If nature is animistic, as it was deemed to be amongst the ancient Greeks and Romans, then every natural event is like a human action, that is, the manifestation of the will of an inherently *unpredictable agent*. And this has two important consequences. Firstly, a crucial point about the natural order as conceived by the sciences is that it is governed by *impersonal* laws of nature. The apple does not choose to fall from the tree. It falls to the ground, accelerating at 32 feet per second squared, whether it wants to or not. There is no room here for free agents behaving according to their own lights, as is the case in animism. The natural order is thus a *determined* order, and this assumed determinism is part and parcel of the predictability of the natural order. Secondly, intervening in the course of nature, as is the wont of the experimental sciences, is from a pagan point of view potentially unethical and often imprudent as these interventions risk incurring the righteous wrath of the aggrieved spirits and gods living in the objects of our experiments. Before a scientist will be willing to put nature to the inquisitorial 'trials and vexations of art', as Bacon has it, she will want to know that she is not trespassing on the rights of a conscious agent. Now animism has not been a popular view in the West for some time, and so this background assumption of the scientific world view will often go entirely unnoticed. But while animism strikes us as a non-starter, that is only because we live in a post-Christian era where non-human agents have been ruthlessly removed from the natural order. The idea that there is one, and only one, God, who exists above all things and prior to all things means that there is *no* god in the local volcano that must be appeased, *no* spirit living in the local well with particular likes and dislikes, *no* mind in the cherry orchard one needs to negotiate with to ensure a good harvest. This de-animated approach to nature amounted to nothing short of atheism as far as the ancient pagans were concerned. And so vociferous was this charge against the early Christians that Augustine was moved to write the *City of God* at least in part to exonerate Christianity's perceived atheism and impiety for the fall of the Roman Empire. The point here though is that a de-animated natural order is an essential element of the mindset in which modern science can even appear possible, and it is not a universal belief system.

A third assumption concerns motivation. Even if the natural order is in principle intelligible, and it is de-animated, it still has to be shown that it is worth investigating. Many societies have failed to undertake systematic studies of the natural order because such studies have not been prioritized. In most societies study and learning amounts to digesting the canonical authorities and texts of one's tradition. It has *not* been about discovering new information about the natural order. Of course book learning was prized in the Latin West as well. But Latin Europe had two 'books': the books of revelation and the so-called 'book' of nature. And there was a theological sanction for the study of both. In Rom. 1.21 we read, 'His invisible attributes, that is to say his everlasting power and deity, have been visible, ever since the world began, to the eye of reason, in the things he has made.' This passage invests the empirical study of nature with theological import. So we hear Roger Bacon saying that experimental sciences are 'useful not only to philosophy but to the knowledge of God' (*Opus Majus*, 587). And William of Conches of the School of Chartres disparages those who denigrate scientific investigation:

> Because they are themselves ignorant of nature's forces and wish to have all men as companions in their ignorance, they are unwilling for anybody to investigate them, but prefer that we believe like peasants and not inquire into the [natural] causes [of things]. However, we say that the cause of everything is to be sought ... but these people ... if they know of anybody so investigating, proclaim him a heretic. (Woods 2012)

Now all three assumptions – that the natural order is subject to the principle of sufficient reason, that it is de-animated and that it is worthy of study – are central to medieval thought, but were not common in the ancient world or in contemporary Asia. Thomas Goldstein sums things up as follows:

> Formulating the philosophical premises: defining the basic concept of the cosmos from which all later specialised sciences were to grow; systematically reconstructing the scientific knowledge of the past and thus placing the coming evolution of Western science on a solid traditional footing – each one of these steps seems so crucial that, taken together, they could only mean one thing: that in a period of fifteen to twenty years, around the middle of the twelfth century, a handful of men were consciously striving to launch the evolution of Western science, and undertook every major step that we needed to achieve that end.[5]

Now, one might ask, if all this is true, why is the Catholic Church's attitude to the sciences one of hostility? But the question is founded on a false premise. Far from being hostile, the Catholic Church has been a patron of the sciences. Indeed, much groundbreaking work in the sciences has actually been conducted by churchmen, although they are rarely celebrated. Who remembers the contributions and careers of Roger Bacon (mathematics, optics, scientific method), Albertus Magnus (biology, psychology, earth sciences), Robert Grossteste (experimental design), Nicole Oresme (application of mathematics to astronomy, early monetary theory), Nicholas Steno (optics, geology, stratigraphy), Luis de Molina (economics), Leonardus Lessius (economics), Francesco Cavalieri (optics, mathematics), Giambattista Ricciole (astronomy), Nicolas Zucchie (inventor of the reflecting telescope), Francesco Grimaldi (history of science, mapping of the moon, optics), Roger Boscovich (atomic theory, mathematics, optics, astronomy), Athanius Kircher (chemistry, geology, Egyptology), Frederick Odenbach (seismology), J. B. Macelwane (seismology), to name only a few? This list of scientific luminaries on its own is enough to establish that there is nothing inimical to the sciences in scholasticism per se.[6]

Do the sciences need metaphysics?

Our second preliminary point has to do with the question as to whether the sciences can do without philosophy, and metaphysics in particular. In the early twentieth century, particularly in the analytic tradition, there was a very strong reaction against the prevailing metaphysics of the time, that of the German Idealists. Moore and Russell began the assault, and their lead eventually culminated in the Vienna Circle and logical positivism, which held that metaphysical claims are literally meaningless. If we are to learn anything of the natural world, they maintained, it would be the sciences – employing nothing more than logic and empirical observation – that would lead the way. Metaphysics, along with most of traditional philosophy, was to be abandoned in favour of conceptual analysis and the examination of the functioning of language.

Now anyone familiar with late nineteenth-century German Idealism is likely to be grateful to the logical positivists, even if they do not share any of the characteristic doctrines of the positivist movement. And it is interesting to note that, even with the passing of logical positivism, there has been no concerted effort to rehabilitate late German Idealism (although Kant and Hegel do remain the subject of serious study). Nonetheless, the logical positivist's dream of relying solely on the sciences to inform us of the workings of the natural order was broken backed from the start, although it did take a while for this point to be fully appreciated. As we saw in Chapter 1, the problem is that logic and empirical observations alone do not provide sufficient resources to determine if a scientific theory is true when it is true, or false when it is false. This means that there is no way of testing scientific theories, because no experiment can be run which will allow one to determine the truth-value of the theory under examination.

The basic point, popularized by Quine (1980) in his extremely influential article 'Two Dogmas of Empiricism' but first made systematically by Duhem (1977) in his *The Aim and Structure of Physical Theory*, is that a scientific statement does not confront experience in isolation. In order to generate a prediction about how events in a physical system will unfold one needs more than the scientific claim one is hoping to test. If I want to test Newton's laws of planetary motion, for example, and I intend to do this by seeing if I can make accurate predictions of the positions of the planetary bodies at some date in the future, I need to assume more than Newton's laws of motion. I need to assume what Duhem calls 'auxiliary hypotheses' and beliefs about the 'initial conditions' of the system under observation, that is, beliefs about the present position of the planets and their velocity, beliefs regarding the reliability of the instruments used to assert these positions, beliefs in the reliability of the mathematics used in the generation of the predictions and so forth. The point of this is that if my prediction about the positions of planetary bodies is *not* borne out by experience I *cannot* infer that Newton's laws of motion are false, for what is falsified by the recalcitrant observation is the combination of Newton's laws, the auxiliary hypotheses and the initial conditions. What the experiment establishes is that something is definitely wrong with this combination of claims, but it does not establish precisely what has gone wrong. The point emphasized by Duhem is that logic and observation alone do not force a scientist to reject a scientific claim if experimental observations do not turn out as expected. The scientist must reject *something* of the initial set of claims, but what he rejects is up to him.[7] Now in practice scientists operate with a set of implicit 'disciplinary matrixes' which serve as a guide as to what should be dropped in such cases; but these are said to be matters of convention, not logic or observation. This has led many to claim that science is not really the objective investigation of reality it purports to be because the rules it follows in the course of its investigations are socially constructed and agreed by a group of historically situated observers.

This is not just an interesting side note concerning the logic of scientific methodology. Part of the rationale for privileging the sciences in our social order over religion, or Marxism or Freudian psychoanalysis or other pseudo-sciences, is the claim that scientific theories can be rigorously tested against experience while religion and pseudo-science cannot. The idea is that because scientific theories can be tested, it makes sense to rely more firmly on them than on the untestable claims of non-scientific discourse. But if the Quine–Duhem hypothesis is right – and there is no real controversy on this point – then the sciences are not what we have taken them to be. This has led to hysterical claims, particularly amongst relativists and postmodernists, that the sciences are on equal footing with religion and voodoo and crystal healing techniques, and that there is no rational ground for privileging the sciences over other traditions from an epistemological point of view.

Fortunately relativism and postmodernism have not deterred scientists from pursuing their research in the usual manner. And when the chips are down most of us still advert to the sciences, when we need authoritative information about the natural order. But the anti-intellectualism of relativism and postmodernism has not been entirely without effect, and that effect has not been entirely benign. It has proved a fertile breeding ground of 'post-truth' politics where every opinion is deemed as 'valid' as any other, where the recommendations of 'experts' are treated as so much chaff, where one can always call on 'alternative facts' if the actual facts don't suit your agenda. A consequence of this development is that we now face the pressing issue of defending our reliance on the sciences as authoritative sources of information regarding the natural order.

Thomas Reid once claimed that philosophers and intellectuals are able to tell that their reasonings have led them astray when their conclusions turn out to be nonsensical and absurd. Just as anyone can tell if they have taken a wrong turn on the way to the Albuquerque when they end up in a coal pit, Reid thought that absurd conclusions would be taken by all as clear evidence that errors had crept into our thinking. But as the most recent relativist/postmodernist episode in Western intellectual history has shown, Reid was overly generous in his judgement of intellectuals. What he failed to appreciate is the extent to which intellectuals are the victims of fashion like anyone else. And if absurd conclusions follow from fashionable premises, then one can mistake an absurdity for an exciting discovery. And one of the most persistent intellectual fashions of the twentieth century was the general stance taken against metaphysics. But if one does not appeal to metaphysical principles, the conclusions most likely to be drawn from the Quine–Duhem hypothesis are precisely those of the relativists and postmodernists. What most failed to appreciate is that the 'disciplinary matrixes' employed in the sciences are not arbitrarily agreed social constructs but often the expression, however inchoate in the mouths of scientists, of implicit metaphysical principles that have been rationally defended by Aristotelians for millennia. Since most scientists do not study metaphysics, and since most scientists share the same implicit metaphysical principles, it is not surprising that these matrices have not been recognized for what they are. In short, the way out of the difficulties generated by the Quine–Duhem thesis is to recognize that science does not operate on logic and observation alone; logic and observation are deployed against a metaphysical background which constrains how one reacts to recalcitrant observations: no need for postmodern hysteria. A little metaphysics will do the trick.

The metaphysical background to the sciences

To illustrate the role of metaphysics in the sciences I will develop an analogy based on Grice's work on conversational implicatures. The point of the analogy is that just as Grice's rules of conversational implicature allow one to glean a speaker's meaning from the literal meaning of their uttered sentences, so implicit reliance on metaphysical principles allows one to glean information about the natural order from controlled experiments. And just as most competent speakers have never explicitly entertained Grice's rules despite relying on them in ordinary conversation, so too most scientists never explicitly entertain the metaphysical principles they employ to glean information from experiments. With this analogy in place we can then go on to consider just what these background assumptions might be. My point will be that the metaphysical principles that allow the scientist to learn from experiments are scholastic, not Humean or Kantian or those of twentieth-century positivism.

A bit of background for those new to Grice is in order: in 'Logic and Conversation' Grice was looking at the general conditions that govern conversations regardless of subject matter. One of his important points in this article has to do with the notion of 'implicature', that is, the ability of a speaker to clearly communicate a meaning to an interlocutor despite that meaning being distinct from the literal meaning of what is said. He asks us to imagine two speakers talking about a mutual friend who has just taken up a new job at a bank. The first speaker asks the second how their friend is getting on in his new job, and receives the reply, 'Oh quite well, I think; he likes his colleagues, and he hasn't been to prison yet.' The first speaker, at this point, is bound to see that something is being implied by this statement, because it is most likely that the second speaker's communicative intention is not merely to impart the factual information that their friend is not in jail. It is likely to be something along the lines of their friend being the sort of person who is likely to fall foul of the law if given the opportunity. Grice's point is that this is implied by what the speaker said, but what the speaker implied is distinct from what the speaker actually said. However, the crucial point for Grice is that the first speaker is able to see the implication despite its not being contained in what is said.

Another Gricean example will serve to illustrate how common this phenomenon is. Speaker A says, 'I am out of petrol.' Speaker B replies, 'There is a garage round the corner.' Now in normal circumstances Speaker A is going to take B's reply to imply that the garage is not far away, that it is open and that it has petrol to sell, despite the fact that B never actually said these things. And, again, Grice's point is that A is quite right to impute these communicative intentions to B despite the fact that B never said them. Now the Gricean project here is to unearth how these conversational implicatures work. How do language users routinely pick up the implications of other language users? And Grice's answer is that ordinary conversations are governed by certain very general, though usually unrecognized, rules or principles. He expresses the main communicative principle as follows: 'Make your conversational contribution such as is required, at the stage at which it occurs, by the accepted purpose or direction of the talk exchange in which you are engaged. One might label this the Cooperative Principle'.[8] The idea is that when two people are conversing there are background commitments, usually unnoticed, such as commitment to the co-operative principle, that we expect the other person to respect. We glean a speaker's communicative intentions from their utterances by assuming that these utterances *do* respect these background commitments *even when they seem to flout them*. It is only because A is assuming that B is respecting the co-operative principle that he can see that B is implying that the garage is not far away, that it is open and that it has petrol. If these things were not true, then B would be providing useless information and no longer respecting the co-operative principle.[9]

Now my reason for including this discussion of Gricean implicatures is that there is a close analogy between our understanding a speaker's meaning and a scientist's interpretation of controlled experiments. The data produced by an experiment, like speaker's utterances, have to be interpreted in the light of certain principles if their 'meaning' is to be appreciated. It is only in the light of the communicative principles that we can move from the literal meaning of the speaker's words to the speaker's actual communicative intention. In experiments, it is only in the light of metaphysical principles that one can interpret the data in order to answer the question the experiment is designed to address. Again, both kinds of principles are so obvious that they never need stating explicitly. This is a fundamental point about metaphysics. The principles of metaphysics are not about some dubious realm of existence beyond or behind experience, but express views that are so utterly banal that most never bother to entertain them, and it is only when a philosopher denies them that one begins to notice. A look at the *design* of scientific experiments will illustrate my point.

The design of scientific experiments

The natural sciences live and die by observations, and particularly by the experiment. As we said, it is precisely because scientific theories can be tested against experience that science is accorded a privileged epistemological status in our social order. This is an important point to recognize about the sciences: it is not so much the theories themselves that attract our respect, for theories are often revised or abandoned entirely in the light of newly acquired empirical data. Rather it is the *methodology* used to support them that really counts. It is because these theories have been tested *in a particular way* that we think it is rational to accept them, if only provisionally. But the problem is that the Quine–Duhem hypothesis seems to undermine this methodology. And it does, *if* one tries to do science with logic and observation alone.

But the sciences do *not* make do with logic and observation alone. And this is clear enough from the fact that not all experiments that meet the logical form that Quine and Duhem deploy to set out their challenge would satisfy the scientist. A considerable amount of scene-setting has to occur before the data of an experiment can be read confidently. This scene-setting is accomplished in large part by observing the rules of experimental design. These rules are extra-logical and extra-observational. But if one combines logic and observation *with* the principles of experimental design, the force of the Quine–Duhem hypothesis is muted, because the pressure of a recalcitrant observation falls more securely on the hypothesis being tested rather than on the initial conditions or the auxiliary hypotheses. But the crucial point here is that the principles of experimental design allow the pressure to build on the hypothesis *only* if one assumes that the fundamental structure of reality is pretty much as the scholastics would have it. In the absence of these metaphysical principles the basics of experimental design are toothless in the face of the Quine–Duhem challenge, primarily because so many assumptions regarding the initial conditions of experiment are of a metaphysical nature. It is at this level that the sciences are deeply committed to scholastic principles.

How is this commitment manifested? Consider the two kinds of empirical study carried out by the sciences. The simpler of the two kinds, the so-called 'observational study', involves gathering observational data about a given phenomenon, and then either simply recording the data, or extrapolating from the observation of a finite number of cases to claims about the entire group. Polls are a familiar example of this kind of study. Pollsters ask a number of individuals for their views on some topic, and then on the basis of this limited sample they draw conclusions about the entire population. Now this pattern of inference was famously problematized by Hume, and every philosopher of science since has had to cope with the so-called 'problem of induction'. We will return to this point shortly in our discussion of experiments, the second kind of empirical study.

Experiments differ from observational studies in that experiments usually involve intervening in some way in the natural order to see if altering something about that order *causes* a change in the response of that order. For example, say I want to know if a new drug should be funded on the NHS. In order to be able to make a sensible judgement about this I need to know if the drug is a cost-effective way of treating an illness. Setting aside the cost issue for now, the first matter to be settled is whether the drug actually brings about, that is, causes, an improvement in the given condition. Now establishing causation is beyond the means of the observational study. Whenever we wish to establish that adding A to System B brings about a change C we must run an experiment. And to improve the reliability of an experiment, certain rules of experiment design have been formalized. It is this end (establishing causal connections) and these rules of experimental design that will occupy our attention here.

Firstly it is important to be clear about the logic underlying the running of an experiment. In the following extended passage we hear the voice of the sciences themselves:

> One assumes that the hypothesis that one desires to test is true. Then one examines the consequences of this assumption in terms of a sampling distribution which depends upon the truth of the hypothesis. If, as determined from the sampling distribution, observed data have a relatively high probability of occurring, the decision is made that the data do not contradict the hypothesis. On the other hand, if the probability of an observed set of data is relatively low when the hypothesis is true, the decision is that the data tend to contradict the hypothesis. Frequently the hypothesis that is tested is stated in such a way that, when the data tend to contradict it, the experimenter is actually demonstrating what it is that he is trying to establish. In such cases the experimenter is interested in being able to reject or nullify the hypothesis being tested.[10]

In a layperson's terms, a hypothesis is a proposed explanation for some state of affairs. I have an explanation for a state of affairs when I know its cause. If I want to test the hypothesis that a new drug is effective in, say, reducing blood pressure, I begin by assuming that the hypothesis is true; I then ask myself what consequences I should expect if patients with high blood pressure were given my drug; I then look to see what the consequences actually are; if they are as expected (because they were deemed highly probable), the hypothesis is not contradicted by the data; but if the consequences were deemed to be unlikely if my hypothesis is true prior to the experiment, then the data do not support the hypothesis.

That is the underlying logic of the experiment. But to improve the reliability of the experiment (i.e. to avoid accepting the hypothesis when it is false, or rejecting it when it is true) the following rules must be observed:

1. Include a large enough sample size so that the results are accurate.
2. Choose subjects that most accurately represent the target population.
3. Assign subjects randomly to treatment groups and control groups.
4. Control for possible confounding variables.
5. Double blind the study to avoid bias.
6. Collect good data.
7. Use proper data analysis.
8. Don't draw conclusions that go beyond the data.

Now it is observance of these rules which constitutes the scene-setting required for experimental data to put pressure on a hypothesis. Let us now ask the question, *What does reality have to be like for this logic and these rules to put pressure on the desired target?* The answer is that it must be very much as the scholastic would have it, and decidedly *not* as a Hume or a Kant would have it.

Consider first the very aim of the experiment – to determine if the drug causes an improvement in the condition of patients. The crucial idea here is *causation*. It is not enough for me to have identified a *correlation* between the drug and an improved condition in patients in order to justify claims that it should be used to treat the condition. I must be able to establish that the improved condition is brought about by the action of the drug in the affected patients. But for this to be possible we must assume that causation is a *real* feature of the natural order, an assumption that most philosophical laypeople accept without question, and, as we see, is at the very heart of the scientific enterprise.

Now causal realism is also at the heart of the scholastic world view. Of course Aristotle recognized more varieties of causation than do most scientists, but efficient causality is the causality in question in experimentation, and it has a central place in the Aristotelian system. Now just what efficient causation amounts to, and whether it is anything real at all, continues to be a matter of considerable discussion amongst philosophers working in the Humean tradition.[11] But the settled scholastic view is that the causal relation is a matter of 'reducing potentiality to actuality'. That is, *A* is a cause of *B* if *A*'s activities make the possibility of *B* a reality. More precisely, efficient causation is the communication of some sort of being to a substance by an agent via an action.[12] To continue with our example of the drug trial, the 'substance' is the patient, the 'agent' is the drug, the 'action' is the effect of the drug on the patient, the 'being communicated' is the property of having a lowered blood pressure. But the broader picture is of a natural order populated with entities with natures (which in turn are due to their form). In virtue of their natures, entities have characteristic dispositions, inclinations or tendencies in virtue of which they can bring about changes in other entities. The ability to bring about a change in another thing is called a 'power', and the corresponding ability to be changed by another thing is called a 'liability'. Efficient causation is the name given to the interactions of these paired potentialities of powers and liabilities. It is the business of the natural sciences to investigate the natural order to identify these pairings. The scientific experiment is simply the most sophisticated method we have yet devised to identify these pairings. This scholastic view of the natural order is thus one of the key 'initial conditions' of any scientific experiment, and is analogous to a Gricean rule of conversational implicature. One will not understand an experiment and its results aright if one does not place the experiment within this framework.

Things are very different if we consider the experiment in the light of Humean empiricism or Kantian constructivism. If one considers the standard reading of Hume on the nature of causation one finds that there is no principled way of drawing the distinction between *mere correlations* of *A*s and *B*s, and *genuine causal relationships* between *A*s and *B*s. And that is because (i) there is no observable difference between cases of *B*s *happening* to follow *A*s, and *B*s *having* to follow *A*s,[13] and (ii) there is no *logical* contradiction in the claim that an *A* was not followed by a *B*, or that a *B* arose in the absence of any cause whatsoever.[14] Hume is left then with his constant conjunction thesis regarding causation: 'We may define cause to be an object followed by another, and where all the objects, similar to the first, are followed by objects similar to the second.' But this regularity thesis provides no way of recognizing the *modal* distinction between an *accidental* connection between *A*s and *B*s (all *A*s just happening to be *B*s) and a relation of *necessitation* of *B*s by *A*s (*A*s causing *B*s), and so cannot recognize the difference between a mere correlation and genuine causation. Hume's point is that we have a tendency to believe that causes necessitate their effects, because we always see *B*s following *A*s; however, this belief in causation is not grounded in observation or logic but is merely a projection of the mind on to things themselves. There is no necessity to be found in the natural order, according to Hume, and so no causation as the scholastic has it. And Kant follows Hume inasmuch as he too denies that causation is to be found in things in themselves. He departs from Hume only by continuing to claim that causes *do* necessitate their effects, but the origin of that necessity is *not* grounded in the natures of things themselves (as scholastics would have it), but in the categories of the human mind. *We humans* are the source of the necessity to be found between causes and their effects, and this is because the phenomenal world is itself *mind dependent*.

Now the *merits* of these various approaches to causation – scholastic, Humean and Kantian – are not our primary concern here. What is important for our purposes is simply to note that the Humean and Kantian approaches do not sit well with the scientific world view because neither gives an account of causation that makes it a mind-independent feature of the natural order. The very fact that controlled experiments are used to test hypotheses, and hypotheses are proposed explanations for states of affairs, and explanations are rooted in a proposed causal relationship between the subject of the hypothesis and the state of affairs to be explained, shows the sciences to be committed to a view of the world that common sense and the scholastics are happy with, but neo-Humeans and neo-Kantians cannot unequivocally accept. The importance of this point cannot be underestimated. For all the 'modernity' of a Hume or a Kant, neither provides a suitable metaphysics for the sciences.

This theme continues once attention turns to the rules governing experiment design. Perhaps the most telling is the first rule regarding sample size. If I want to establish that *A*s cause *B*s in systems *C*, it is not enough to observe a few *A*s, *B*s and *C*s. But nor am I told that I must observe *all* *A*s, *B*s and *C*s. I am told that I must observe a sufficient number of *A*s, *B*s and *C*s to be able to say something that will safely apply to *all* *A*s, *B*s and *C*s. In the language of statistics, this is the inferential move from observations made of a *sample* to claims about a *population*. But the crucial point for our present purposes is that experimental method *assumes* that such an inferential move can be made legitimately, that is, that on the basis of observations of a finite sample of *A*s, say, one *can* safely reach conclusions about *all* *A*s. It is because the scientist feels confident that she can speak about all *A*s, *B*s and *C*s that the data turned up in the experiment can be taken to speak to the truth or falsity of the hypothesis that *A*s cause *B*s in *C* (if the other rules of experimental design are also followed). But as any philosophy undergraduate will tell you, this inference pattern was rejected by Hume. There is no *logical* guarantee that the population will resemble the sample *regardless of size*, and since I haven't been able to observe all the individuals of the population I can't reach a conclusion about the entire population on the basis of purely *empirical* evidence either. Again Hume's point is that one cannot get as far as one would like, epistemologically speaking, on the basis of logic and observations alone. This so-called 'problem of induction' has been perhaps the greatest challenge to empiricism and its claim to be the philosophy of the sciences.[15]

Now consider the scholastic position with respect to the inferential move from sample to population. The first point to recognize is that the scholastics would accept Hume's assessment of how far one can get on the basis of logic and observation alone. The fact is that one *cannot* get from sample to population safely on these slim foundations, and so science itself cannot be grounded on these foundations alone. What is required is a little metaphysics. And the necessary metaphysics was introduced in the previous chapter in our discussion of the problem of universals and the problem of change.

As we saw, Aristotelians draw a distinction between an object's matter and form. In virtue of its matter, an object is a distinct individual. In virtue of having a *form*, an object has a *nature*. That nature endows an entity with certain properties or characteristics in virtue of which it is able to have effects on other things, and be affected by other things in characteristic ways. That is, entities in the natural order have powers and liabilities, dispositions and inclinations specific to and rooted in their kind. This is a matter of metaphysics.

Now the powers and liabilities of an object *determine* what it does and can do, and what higher level properties it might have. This too is a matter of metaphysics. But this determination is only 'for the most part', as Aristotle puts it. There is a degree of variability in the instances of most kinds, and so what is true of one instance need not be true of all. But, and this is the crucial bit, *the degree of variability in a kind is restricted by the common form*. And this has a significant implication for experimental science: *one can be more confident about the properties of a population as a whole than one can be about the properties of any one individual of that population*. This is the idea behind the so-called 'Law of Large Numbers', and what Keynes called the 'Stability of Statistical Frequencies', both of which are 'absolutely essential for ... Statistical Induction'.[16] The idea is that the random variability in the individuals of a population cancels out as one increases the sample size. This assumption is a crucial initial condition one must assume to be in place if an experiment is to tell us anything about the hypothesis being tested. And this initial condition is to be expected *if* one is operating within the scholastic metaphysical framework. It *does* make sense to think that on the basis of a proper sampling of a population one *can* confidently reach conclusions about the properties of the population as a whole, *if* one accepts the metaphysical notion of 'form'. Indeed it is *only* in such a framework that the frequency theory of probability, vital to the design of an experiment, is at all sensible, for it is only the notion of 'form' which allows for variability while keeping it with fairly restricted bounds.[17] The scholastic theory of form then is another key 'initial condition' of any scientific experiment, and is analogous to a Gricean rule of conversational implicature. One will not understand an experiment and its results aright if one does not place the experiment within this context. But again, the merits of these views on probability are not our main point. The take-home message is that, once again, scholasticism and the sciences are on the same page, while Humean metaphysics leaves the scientific experiment hamstrung.

A few words on the remaining rules of experimental design will drive the message home. The scientist is enjoined to choose subjects at random to ensure an accurate representation of the target population, to then assign them randomly to treatment groups and control groups and to ensure that the study is double blind. These three rules are there to minimize the possibility of a skewed sample, and to limit the possibility of bias in the study, either on the part of the subjects (patients, say) or on the part of those running the experiment itself. Now the very notion of 'bias' presupposes the possibility of misrepresentation. And, again, this concern make senses if one thinks that the goal of the experiment is to identify *mind-independent* causal relations in things themselves. The experiment has to be designed in such a way as to ensure that the mental states of the participants in the study do not contaminate the data. The hopes and expectations of the experimenter are perhaps the paradigmatic case of potentially distorting mental states. The so-called 'placebo effect' in patients also has to be controlled for. But the key idea here is that the experiment is intentionally designed to separate off as much as possible the influence of the mind in our recording and reading of the data from the natural order. Now the scientist would not go to all this trouble if he did not think that it was possible at least in principle to gather 'clean data'. But this runs counter to neo-Kantian constructivist ideas, according to which the 'natural order' is itself in some sense a social construct. According to social constructivists all data is 'theory-laden', a thesis which undercuts the mind independence of the natural order. And of course it fails to fit with Hume's thesis that causation is imputed to things in virtue of our habitually seeing causes and effects following each other in the nature of things. Again, our point is not to enter into the merits of these views, but simply to point out that these principles of experimental design make sense if one agrees with the scholastic that the natural order is a mind-independent system of entities whose natures we hope to discover via empirical study.

Consider next the rule of controlling for confounding variables. The idea here is that the world is a causally messy place. While *A*s might cause *B*s in the ordinary run of things, there might be other factors at play in the natural order that can disrupt this normal causal relationship. Such disrupting factors, sometimes called 'finks', 'antidotes' or 'masks', have to be controlled for in order to be confident that one has not missed a genuine causal link between *A*s and *B*s. Or it might be that we are mistaken in thinking that *A*s cause *B*s, and it is rather that some hidden factor *C* is causing *both A*s and *B*s. It is to deal with a causally complicated world that scientists try to control for possible confounding variables to be able to justify their hypothesis that it is *A*s causing *B*s and not something else. Now this is precisely the sort of picture that makes sense according to the scholastic world view, for the natural order is replete with inter-connected lines of causation which often interfere with each other. This is one reason why things happen only 'for the most part' in the natural order. But the point for our present purposes is that, again, metaphysical commitments have to be implicitly called upon in order to make an inventory of all the likely confounding factors.

For example, does the scientist believe that causation can happen at a distance? If not, what is the basis of that claim? If they do, how does the scientist control for possible interfering factors emanating from distant regions of the universe? The scholastics (in)famously deny action at a distance as inconsistent with their understanding of efficient causation, and so they are in a position to rule out possible confounding factors from far off entities on principled grounds. And what applies to regions of space also applies to time. Scientists tend not to take seriously the suggestion that future events might influence the results of their experiment. This would involve belief in the reality of the future, or belief in backwards causation, that is, the idea that events that are later in time can cause events that happened prior to them. Given that many scientists and contemporary metaphysicians sign up to the block theory of time – the view that all moments of time are equally real – it is not obvious how they can rule out causal influences from the future. Scholastics, being principled presentists, need not worry about interference in today's experiments by agents acting in the future. But they do so explicitly on metaphysical grounds. The point for us is that if the scientist discounts possible interference from the future in their experiment, they can do so only if they have signed up to a metaphysics which denies such things are possible. Controlling for confounding variables is the step where so many further metaphysical claims come into play that normally pass entirely unnoticed, but are crucial if the data of an experiment is to put pressure on a hypothesis. And in both these cases, that is, action at a distance and action from the future, the scholastic metaphysical framework provides grounds for ruling these out.

But perhaps the basic point of this section on experimental design has to do with the final rule: do not draw conclusions that go beyond the data. Now in the strict sense this rule cannot be right, because as Hume has shown, and as Quine and Duhem have underlined, one *has* to go beyond the brute data if one is to establish anything about causal relations in the natural order. But we *can* go beyond the brute data *if* we allow ourselves to employ scholastic metaphysical principles, just as in understanding our fellow conversationalists we must frequently go beyond the literal meaning of their utterances to understand what they are trying to communicate. Humean empiricism, Kantian constructivism, relativism and postmodernism afford the sciences no such move.

Conclusion

We have seen (i) that the background assumptions that need to be in place before the scientific investigation of the natural order makes sense are present in the thought of the Latin medieval Europeans; (ii) that much significant first-order scientific work has been carried out by churchmen; (iii) that some extra-logical and extra-observational principles are necessary if the Quine–Duhem hypothesis is to be overcome and experiments are to put pressure on hypotheses being tested; (iv) that the standard rules of experimental design do allow pressure to be brought to bear on hypotheses; (v) that, however, these rules succeed only if one presupposes metaphysical principles of a scholastic flavour. The most basic of these principles concerns the mind independence of the natural order, an order populated with entities with repeatable essential natures that endow them with real causal powers and liabilities. Scholastic ideas are deeply embedded in the scientific world view. If scientific experiments matter, so does scholasticism.

CHAPTER THREE

The meta-philosophy of scholasticism

So who were the scholastics, and what were they up to? This chapter and the next answer these questions by focusing on their collective project and the methods used to prosecute it. A focus on project and method is enlightening because one's meta-philosophy determines the broad outlines of a philosopher's thought. To fix ideas I will draw a sharp contrast between the scholastic project and what came to replace it, namely Cartesianism. But the point as far as the broader thesis of this work is concerned is that the scholastic project, or something structurally very much like it, remains viable and attractive today.

> The greatest philosophers have been the greatest, and most self-conscious, methodologists; indeed, I am tempted to regard the fact as primarily accounting for their greatness as philosophers.[1]

Introduction

So far much has been said in this book about the social order of modern Western societies, about common sense and about the sciences. The idea has been to show that scholasticism has important links to things that clearly matter. But it is now time to start looking directly at scholasticism itself. After all, the primary aim of this work is to spark an interest in scholasticism amongst those who never imagined that anything of lasting philosophical significance might have occurred during the Middle Ages. This is no small task. Like Hobbes, most labour under the false impression that 'the Schoolmen' were purveyors of a 'dark' and 'vain' philosophy expressed in 'insignificant Traines of strange or barbarous words' about obscure metaphysical entities justified only by empty ratiocinations and verbal disputations carried out under the suspicious eye of an ever vigilant Church.[2] Unfortunately this attitude was set in stone by the first great modern historian of philosophy. In his *Historia Critica Philosophiae* of 1742, Johann Jakob Brucker, having limited access to the works of the scholastics themselves, simply repeated the diatribes of scholasticism's renaissance and early modern detractors. His history was a great success, going through many editions and being translated into English in 1791. It licenced the contemptuous attitude to scholasticism that has hitherto been the obligatory pose amongst philosophers with no familiarity with the period.

Now I hope enough has been said in the opening chapters of this book to win scholasticism a retrial. As Victor Cousin and his eclectic school began to show as far back as the mid-1800s – and as has been demonstrated repeatedly ever since – the scholastics were highly sophisticated metaphysicians, logicians, epistemologists, cognitive psychologists, ethicists, economists and political theorists, and there is much to be gained by a sustained study of the period. And far from being monolithic defenders of the faith, who 'resolve of their Conclusions before they know their Premises',[3] the period is replete with colourful characters who differed significantly, and often heatedly, on important matters.

So who were the scholastics, and what were they up to? It is the business of this chapter to begin to answer this question. But I will not be focusing on particular figures such as Aquinas or Ockham, but rather on the shared philosophical framework within which their work was carried out. I will make a start by focusing on the defining feature of *any* philosophical system, namely, its *meta-philosophy*. By 'meta-philosophy' I mean one's 'philosophy of philosophy'. And the key ingredients of a meta-philosophy are (i) an account of the philosophical enterprise per se and (ii) an inventory of the techniques to be used in the prosecution of that enterprise. The reason for focusing on these 'meta' issues in the first instance is that nothing determines the subsequent trajectory of a philosopher's thought more decisively than their overarching project and methodology. Indeed nothing is more central to a philosopher's self-image. In fact it is probably not too much of an exaggeration to say that once a meta-philosophy is in place the rest is simply a matter of drawing out the implications. For one's meta-philosophy places constraints on what one can take to be a genuine philosophical issue in the first place inasmuch as one will chauvinistically regard a question, topic or task as philosophical only if it is amenable to treatment using one's favoured method or methods. Certainly a philosopher is unlikely to spend much time on a task if they do not believe they have the means necessary to carry out the project successfully. And while it is true that a philosopher's meta-philosophy will not necessarily determine the specific answer they give to a particular question, at the very least it will limit the range of possible solutions they are going to consider worthy of serious attention. For all of these reasons, a philosopher's conscious or unconscious decisions regarding project and methods are particularly momentous.

There is another reason for focusing of meta-philosophical issues here. Firstly, the scholastic meta-philosophy lies behind the account of philosophy given in Chapter 1 of this book. To be clear, the philosophical agenda laid out in Chapter 1 is, in effect, a modern-day scholastic agenda. Secondly, the scholastic vision of philosophy was abandoned with the advent of Descartes. Descartes's historical significance is that he institutionalized a radical change in philosophy's self-image. This was a fateful transition for the discipline. Comparing and contrasting these two images of philosophy brings out just what is at issue in the transition from scholasticism to early modernity and beyond. Appreciating the differences between the scholastics and Descartes on methodology is the main order of business in this chapter. But the point as far as the broader thesis of this work is concerned is that the scholastic project, or something structurally very much like it, remains viable and attractive today.

Who were the scholastics?

To understand scholasticism it has to be put in context. In particular one has to recall that the Middle Ages and the scholastic project itself were born out of the wreckage of the Roman Empire. As the Empire collapsed, and the social order that had been in place for centuries fell away, 'barbarian' peoples from Northern Europe came to settle in regions that had previously been under Roman control. These barbarian migrations brought Vandals, Goths, Visigoths, Ostrogoths, Franks and Normans, and a host of other peoples unfamiliar with the ways of the ancient world, deep into the heart of the former Empire.

Now it is not uncommon for the victors in war to come to emulate the vanquished foe. The Romans themselves conquered Greece, but continually found themselves emulating their Greek masters in the arts, literature, the sciences and, of course, philosophy. This pattern was repeated. Although the centre of civilizational gravity gradually shifted north in the Middle Ages from Athens, Alexandria, Antioch and Carthage to Canterbury, Paris, Oxford and Cologne, the unlettered victors were deeply impressed with the cultural achievements of the Romans, and in due course they set about recovering and then assimilating the wisdom of the ancient world.

These Northern Europeans are the stock from which scholasticism grew, and this process of recovery and assimilation was the first stage in its long development. Pieper elaborates on this point rather nicely as follows:

> Medieval philosophy ... was an affair of those peoples who penetrated into the ancient world from the North. [These] young peoples ... considered it their task to master and assimilate the accumulated body of tradition they found, including the enormous harvest of patristic theology as well as the wisdom of the ancient world. [And it is] only in the light of this fact [that] can we understand one decisive trait of medieval thinking: its 'scholarly' aspect – to which, after all, the name 'scholasticism' refers. Truly to understand scholasticism, we must bear in mind that it was above all an unprecedented process of learning, a scholarly enterprise of enormous proportions that went on for several centuries.[4]

So the first step in the scholastic project was the recovery and assimilation of the intellectual heritage of the ancient world from the wreckage of the Empire. And that heritage had three outstanding elements: (i) the patristic commentaries on the Hebrew and Christian Bibles, (ii) Roman law and (iii) Greek philosophy.

This scholarly activity was a significant challenge, and of immense historical significance in and of itself. But a different sort of challenge followed quickly on the first, namely, *synthesizing the recovered material into a coherent system of thought*. For the patristic heritage did not always sit easily side by side with works of the philosophers. That is, the scholastics came to recognize the challenge of synthesizing Athens with Jerusalem, reason with faith, philosophy with religion. And it is here that we begin to see the core of the scholastic project. Christianity had been the official religion of the Empire, and so it enjoyed pride of place in the commitments of the scholastics. But the splendour and authority of the ancient world and its leading philosophical figures was such that it was very difficult to reject a Plato or an Aristotle even if they appeared to contradict religious teaching. A barbarian does not throw away any treasure of the ancient world lightly.

The desire to preserve philosophy also had a purely theological foundation. The main task of those who considered themselves primarily theologians was to develop a systematic theology out of the Hebrew and Christian Bibles. But the Old Testament is the story of the people of Israel, and the New Testament gospels give us four versions of the life of Jesus. These texts are *not* theological treatises. These narrative texts are, of course, suggestive; but they do not contain developed reflections on their own contents, and they certainly do not offer any obvious solutions to the problem posed by their many internal contradictions. It became tempting then to think that one might avail oneself of the tools of the pagan philosophers in drawing out the implications of these narratives and developing a coherent theological system. And it is here that we find the first point of method in scholasticism. The scholastics were those theologians who believed that philosophy could play precisely this role. Rosemann puts this well:

> The New Testament, while fundamentally narrative in structure, encourages theological reflection, that is to say, the penetration of the faith by means of reason. First and foremost, such theological reflection faces the task of demonstrating the unity of God's revelation in the Old and New Testaments. This is a task of reconciling, and synthesising, two sets of divinely inspired texts. The use of non-Christian concepts and ideas is portrayed as legitimate, so long as no attempt is made to reduce the foolishness

> of the cross to mere natural reason – and, of course, so long as these concepts and ideas can themselves be reconciled and synthesised with the Christian tradition. In these three elements – intellectual penetration of the faith, systematization of the texts upon which it is based, and dialogue with non-Christian thought – we already find the seeds of … the Scholastic method.[5]

So in answer to our question 'Who were the scholastics?', we can say that the scholastics were thinkers who worked, directly or indirectly, on understanding the faith, of synthesizing that faith in a way that does justice to the Old and New Testaments, and employing philosophy in the prosecution of this project. Early patristic roots of this approach were already there in Augustine, but the heavy lifting on the project was performed by the outstanding figures of scholasticism: Anselm of Canterbury, Peter Abelard, John of Salisbury, Alexander of Hales, Albertus Magnus, Thomas Aquinas, Bonaventure, Henry of Ghent, Giles of Rome, Duns Scotus, William of Ockham, Francisco de Vitoria, Francisco Suarez, to name only a few.

But as I pointed out in Chapter 1, not all medieval thinkers were scholastics, and so one cannot equate medieval philosophy with scholasticism without mischaracterizing the period. As we shall see in a moment, the philosopher of choice amongst scholastics was Aristotle. If Augustine was their primary source in theology, Aristotle was 'The Philosopher'. But not all medieval thinkers accepted the main lines of Aristotelian metaphysics, and not all accepted orthodox Church doctrine. Moreover, many rejected the project of faith seeking understanding itself, either because they rejected the need of philosophy altogether, or, conversely, because they thought that reason could make do without the faith, or because they thought that ultimately reason had very little to say about the faith after all. But these medieval thinkers did not attract the kind of following the scholastics themselves enjoyed amongst the intelligentsia.[6] And one of the reasons for their failure to become mainstream intellectual movements is that these non-scholastic endeavours required abandoning some important element or other of the intellectual heritage of the ancient world. The scholastics were those who refused to follow the likes of the Latin Averroists in rejecting the patristic heritage entirely; they also refused to follow the likes of Tertullian who rejected pagan philosophy out of hand,

and they refused to lapse into an anti-intellectual mysticism that declined to confront the fault lines in the ancient heritage. The scholastics were very aware of the tensions to be found in the intellectual legacy of the ancient world, but they resolved both to think through those tensions with the rigour of the philosophers *and* to preserve as much of the ancient heritage as possible. To throw away anything would be to risk losing some important truth. The task of synthesis was therefore paramount. And for this task they found methodological guidance in Aristotle.

Aristotle's aporetic method

Aristotle would have recognized immediately the nature of the scholastic challenge. The logical shape of the scholastic project is quintessentially philosophical, or 'dialectical' as Aristotle would have said. Aristotle does not discuss his method explicitly in the kind of detail we find in Descartes, but there are plenty of programmatic remarks scattered throughout his works from which a method can be constructed. Perhaps most important is the passage which immediately precedes his discussion of akrasia in the *Nicomachean Ethics*. He writes,

> We must, as in all other cases, set the observed facts before us and, after first discussing the difficulties, go on to prove, if possible the truth of all the common opinions about these affections of the mind, or, failing this, of the greater number and the most authoritative; for if we both refute the objections and leave the common opinions undisturbed, we shall have proved the case sufficiently. (Bk. VII. Ch. 1, 1145b2–7)

This is a condensed summary of Aristotle's aporetic approach to philosophical problems. On this picture of philosophical activity one begins with a puzzle or 'aporia'. The reader was introduced to two such aprorias, the problem of universals and the problem of change, in Chapter 2. An aporia arises, says Aristotle, 'when we reason on both sides [of a question] and it appears to us that everything can come about either way'. This produces 'a state of aporia about which of the two ways to take up' (*Topics*,VI, 145b16–20). An aporia is really the discovery of a tension in beliefs or lines of thought that the philosopher finds attractive. The distinctly philosophical challenge is to find a way of overcoming the at least prima facie contradictions in beliefs one is already inclined to accept. So, in the case currently before him, Aristotle begins with the observation that akrasia seems to be a common fact of life attested to by ordinary folk. But he notes that Socrates, a reputable authority, maintains that akrasia is impossible. So the question arises: is akrasia possible? And since there are good reasons on both sides of the question, a state of puzzlement arises. The task of the philosopher is to solve the puzzle while respecting as many of the initial beliefs as possible. If one can remove the puzzlement while respecting most of the initial beliefs, or at least the most authoritative, then one will have 'proved the case sufficiently'. But the important point for our present purposes is that Aristotle's discussion of akrasia provides in miniature a model of the challenge facing the scholastics: lines of thought one is inclined to accept appear to be contradictory or otherwise in tension. The task of the philosopher, the task of the scholastics, is to solve the puzzle while respecting as many of the authorities of the ancient world as possible.

Aristotle adopts this aporetic approach to philosophical questions in all areas of his work. Nowhere is this more apparent than in the *Metaphysics*. After a historical survey of his predecessors (in Alpha and Alpha the Lesser) Aristotle sets out at the beginning of the third book (Beta) a number of aporia that arise in the context of metaphysics. The task of the metaphysician, says Aristotle, is to solve these puzzles, and no progress is possible in metaphysics if one is not fully aware of precisely these puzzles. An extended passage is worth quoting in full:

> With a view to the science under investigation [metaphysics] we must attack first those puzzles which must first be investigated. … Now for those who wish to investigate the truth it is worthwhile to ponder these difficulties well. For the subsequent study of truth is nothing else than the solution of earlier problems. For it is impossible to untie a knot without knowing it. But a perplexity on the part of the mind makes this evident in regard to the matter at hand; for insofar as the mind is perplexed, to that extent it experiences something similar to men who are bound; for in both cases it is impossible to move forward. For this reason, then, it

> is first necessary to consider all the difficulties and the reasons for them. ... [This is also necessary] for another reason, namely, that those who make investigations without first recognising the problems are like those who do not know where they ought to go. Again, one would not even know when he finds the thing which he is seeking [and when not]; for the goal is not evident to such a man but is evident to one who previously discussed the difficulties. (*Metaphysics*, Book III, Ch. 1 995a24–995b2)

Now this is the next element of the meta-philosophy of the scholastics. For all the differences to be found amongst the key figures, one can group them together in a single stable of thinkers in that they all take aporia arising out the prima facie tensions found between the Old and New Testaments, and between these and philosophy, particularly Aristotle, as their point of departure. Moreover, they all accept that a response to an aporia that preserves as much of the initial material as possible is to be preferred to one that requires abandoning a recognized authority, be it patristic or philosophical. Peter Lombard's *Sentences* and Peter Abelard's *Sic et Non* are perfect early examples of this approach. In both works the authors deliberately and explicitly set out the contradictory views of authorities on specific questions. This then sets the theological agenda – solve *these* aporia. This is entirely as Aristotle's aporetic method would have it.[7]

Now before entering further into the details of this meta-philosophy, and before suggesting that the logical shape of the project remains viable today, it would be worth contrasting it at this point with the meta-philosophy of Descartes.

Descartes on method

One way of clarifying the meta-philosophy of the scholastics is to compare and contrast it with another. Since the meta-philosophy of the scholastics gave way to that of Descartes, who sought to overcome scholasticism, and because readers are likely to be familiar with the main outlines of Cartesianism, contrasting the father of modern philosophy with Aristotle on points of method is particularly helpful.

No one appreciated the importance of method more than Descartes. In his *Rules for the Direction of the Mind* he goes so far as to claim that 'it is far better never to contemplate investigating the truth about any matter than to do so without a method' (Vol. 1, p. 16). Descartes agonized at length over questions of method, and the upshot of these reflections were as influential on the subsequent course of philosophical history as any particular thesis he defended on what one might call 'first level' philosophical questions. Part of the explanation for Descartes's concern with method is no doubt captured in Aquinas's dictum: *Parvus error in principe, maximus est in fine*:[8] a small error at the beginning of a project or endeavour ensures that the final product will be vitiated through and through. And since one's first moves are dictated by one's method, a fault in one's method guarantees disaster.

Let us start then with a reminder of the main lines of Descartes's method, and the philosophical framework or mindset in which this method makes sense. This framework can then be contrasted point by point with that of Aristotle, thereby bringing into stark relief the differences between the last great philosopher of antiquity and the father of modern philosophy.

In his *Rules for the Direction of the Mind* and *Discourse on the Method* Descartes's sets out with admirable clarity and frankness the rules according to which he conducted his philosophical business. This is well-worn territory, and I will not attempt anything like a complete study of the method in all its details. For our purposes it is enough simply to remind ourselves of these rules as Descartes presents them.[9]

Descartes lays out the key elements of his meta-philosophy in Part Two of the *Discourse*. He begins by noting that works 'produced by various different craftsmen' are rarely as perfect as those made by one man (p. 116). Just as many cooks spoil the broth, so many thinkers engaged on a common project are sure to produce an inelegant hodgepodge. It is best then for the philosopher to think alone, to develop their philosophical thoughts in isolation without the interference or help of others. But this raises a problem because all of one's thoughts, opinions, beliefs and customs, at least in the first instance, are adopted uncritically from the society of which one is a member. It is only natural in one's early years to take for granted what one is told by various figures of authority. So, at least in the first instance, one cannot think on one's own because one's very thoughts are the common property of the culture in which one has been raised. Descartes's solution is to try to set aside all the beliefs acquired during this enculturation process. He writes,

> Regarding the opinions to which I had hitherto given credence, I thought that I could not do better than undertake to get rid of them, all at one go, in order to replace them afterwards with better ones, or with the same ones once I had squared them with the standards of reason. (p. 117)

The upshot of Descartes's resolution to think on one's own is that he has to start from scratch. Rather than relying on 'old foundations' and 'old principles' accepted before he had attained the age of reason, he must find his own foundations, or, if he adopts old foundations, he will do so only once they have passed his, rather than anyone's else's, scrutiny.

Since Descartes is taking on an extremely heavy intellectual responsibility, and one he imagines will have practical no less than theoretical consequences, it is unsurprising that he is concerned about the possibility of error. He then comments that he has been impressed by the fact that logic, geometry and algebra alone amongst the subjects he has studied have generated results that are absolutely certain. Therefore he decides that these three arts 'ought to contribute something to my plans' (p. 119). In fact he explicitly develops a philosophical method that incorporates the best features of those employed in logic, geometry, and algebra. He then identifies four rules he believes does just this, and he resolves 'never to fail to observe them' (p. 120).

The four rules are worth quoting in full:

> The first was never to accept anything as true if I did not have evident knowledge of its truth: that is, carefully to avoid precipitate conclusions and preconceptions, and to include nothing more in my judgments that what presented itself to my mind so clearly and distinctly that I had no occasion to doubt it.
>
> The second, to divide each of the difficulties I examined into as many parts as possible and as may be required in order to resolve them better.
>
> The third, to direct my thoughts in an orderly manner, by beginning with the simplest and most easily known objects in

> order to ascend little by little, step by step, to knowledge of the most complex, and by supposing some order even among objects that have no natural order of precedence.
>
> And the last, throughout to make enumerations so complete, and reviews so comprehensive, that I could be sure of leaving nothing out. (p. 120)

Descartes expresses great confidence in these rules.[10] And he then takes a further step:

> Those long chains composed of very simple and easy reasonings, which geometers customarily use to arrive at their most difficult demonstrations, had given me occasion to suppose that all the things which can fall under human knowledge are interconnected in the same way. And I thought that, provided we refrain from accepting anything as true which is not, and always keep to the order required for deducing one thing from another, there can be nothing too remote to be reached in the end or too well hidden to be discovered. (p. 120)

Now, given that everything that falls within the purview of human knowledge can be reached in this manner, and given that error is entirely avoidable as long as one scrupulously obeys the rules already laid down; it is understandable that Descartes goes on to make one further claim regarding his method, namely, that no other method is required. Descartes says that he does not 'restrict the method to any particular subject matter', for he hopes 'to apply it usefully to the problems of the other sciences' (p. 121). This method, Descartes claims, is the only method he will use when engaged in the business of philosophy.[11]

That Descartes is serious about this method is evident from the fact that he follows it in all important respects in the course of his first-order philosophical efforts. A quick reminder of the general outline of the *Mediations* is enough to satisfy ourselves on this score. In line with his plan, in the *First Meditations* Descartes resolves to put aside all his beliefs about which any doubt is possible. At the beginning of the *Second Meditations* he identifies a belief that he can hold with absolute certainty, a belief that will serve as the foundational belief of his system (in accordance with the first rule). Then, building upon the cogito and the clear and distinct rule (in accordance with the first and third rules), he begins his quest for knowledge by focusing on epistemologically accessible objects before moving on to those that are more challenging (again in accordance with the third rule). So he starts with his own nature as a thinking thing (since his mind is more accessible epistemologically speaking than his body) before moving on to consider the existence and nature of God. Finally he turns to the nature of the external world. At all times he is conscientious in his observance of the fourth rule, namely, to take account of everything that might have a bearing on the truth of the claims he is prepared to accept.

As noted at the outset, this material will be familiar to anyone who has been introduced to Descartes. The details of the method can be commented on at length, but this outline suffices for our present purposes. At issue for us is the contrast between Aristotle and Descartes.

Aristotle versus Descartes

The picture of philosophical activity at work in Aristotle could hardly be further removed from Descartes's. It is worth going through these differences carefully in order to fully appreciate the distance travelled between the last great philosopher of antiquity with the father of modern philosophy.

Firstly, note the difference in starting point. Both begin with a recognition of perplexity inasmuch as neither knows what to think about a particular issue. But from here on our heroes take radically different paths. Descartes asserts that in order to make any headway one must begin by laying aside all prejudices, in effect to start from scratch from foundational beliefs about which one can be absolutely certain. The hope is that once these foundations have been laid, he will be able to draw out the implications of these beliefs, and, in due course, an answer to his original question will be found amongst these implications. Moreover, as we have seen, the clear message from Descartes is that this effort is best conducted on one's own.

Aristotle's first moves are very different. The first step in Aristotle's view is not to lay aside one's prejudices. In fact it is quite the reverse. Aristotle begins by gathering all the respectable views that have been expressed on the issue in question. The respectable views, 'endoxa' as he calls them, are those views accepted by everyone, or by most people, or at least by the recognized authorities. The idea is that with these views clearly before him he can then begin to understand the origin of the perplexity – for from this position one can begin to see that there are good reasons for holding different views on the question at hand. The philosopher's task then is to remove the perplexity while giving due attention to the pressures that brought the perplexity about in the first place. There is nothing here about starting from self-evident principles on which one builds a system of belief. Moreover, there is no question of the philosopher working in isolation. As with Socrates, Aristotle is quite clear about the fact that philosophy is a group activity. He writes,

> Theoretical, i.e., speculative knowledge of truth is in one sense difficult and in another, easy. An indication of this is found in the fact that, while no one can attain an adequate knowledge of it, *all men together do not fail*, because each one is able to say something true about nature. And while each one individually contributes nothing or very little to the truth, still as a result of the combined efforts of all a great amount of truth becomes known. (*Metaphysics*, Alpha the Lesser, chapter 1, emphasis added)

Note too the difference in the degree of certainty required by both philosophers. Descartes hopes to arrive at his answers to philosophical questions by deriving answers deductively from more basic premises which are themselves either deduced from more basic premises or self-evident in themselves. In this way Descartes's answers are to have all the certainty enjoyed by theorems in geometry. Aristotle requires no such degree of certainty. As he says, if the aporia can be solved while leaving most of the original beliefs intact, or if not all, then most of them, or at least the most authoritative, then the matter is proved sufficiently. There is no question here of beginning from self-evident axioms and deducing answers in the manner of the geometer. And the reason for this, according to Aristotle, is that the demand for certainty associated with deductive reasoning is appropriate in some contexts, like geometry, but not in others. For one must adjust the degree of certainty one seeks to the subject matter under discussion. Aristotle makes this point clearly as follows:

> Our study will be adequately treated if it is investigated according to the nature of the subject matter. The same certitude should not be sought in all discussions just as the same exactness should not be expected in all the productions of art ... the student ought to take whatever is taught, for it is proper to an educated man to look for as much certitude in each study as the nature of the subject permits. It approximates the same thing to allow a mathematician to use rhetorical arguments and to demand conclusive demonstrations from a rhetorician. (*Nicomachean Ethics*, Book I, chapter 1)

Aristotle is quite clear that the degree of certainty sought in mathematics via deductive reasoning is *not* to be had in philosophy per se. As is clear from the opening remarks of the *Topics*, it is *dialectical*, not demonstrative, reasoning that is characteristic of the philosophical sciences. Dialectical reasoning, that is, the reasoning we engage in when we begin with opinions that are generally accepted, and then 'raise searching difficulties on both sides of a subject [to] detect more easily the truth and error about the several points that arise' – this dialectical reasoning is distinctly philosophical as opposed to mathematical (*Topics*, Book I, chapter 2). Dialectical reasoning is also distinctly philosophical because it is used to arrive at

> the ultimate bases of the principles used in the several sciences. For it is impossible to discuss them at all from the principles proper to the particular science in hand, seeing that the principles are the *prius* of everything else. It is through the opinions generally held on the particular points that these have to be discussed. (Aristotle *Topics*, Book I, Ch. 2)

Aristotle takes these points to be obvious, but he is aware that some demand demonstrations of everything. As though chiding Descartes he writes, 'Not to know of what things one should demand a demonstration, and of what things one should not, argues want of education' (*Metaphysics*, Gamma, chapter 4).

These points of difference between Aristotle and Descartes lead to others. To follow his stated rules Descartes must begin from what is epistemologically unassailable, and then move from these allegedly firm foundations to more challenging issues. This means that Descartes has to start all his reasonings from what is immediately accessible to him, and this he takes to be the contents of his own mind. He then faces the challenge of building an entire world view on these slim beginnings, a challenge that many have taken up since Descartes. Aristotle faces no such challenge. He does not have to infer an external world and other minds from the immediate contents of consciousness because he begins not with the contents of his own mind but with 'endoxa', and these already place Aristotle securely in the world of common sense.

The condemnations of 1277

An obvious question at this point is, What happened? Why is the philosophical project of Descartes so different from that of Aristotle? And why did the philosophical mainstream eventually follow Descartes's lead rather than remaining true to Aristotle?

The answers to these questions are pivotal for one's understanding of the history of philosophy. I have dealt with this topic at length elsewhere, so a brief recap of key events will suffice here.[12] The gist of the story is that the scholastic project of Faith seeking Understanding presupposes that human beings can illuminate or penetrate the faith using the 'natural light of reason'. In practice, relying on reason amounted to deploying the most sophisticated philosophical system available, namely, that of Aristotle. But by the mid-thirteenth century it was becoming clear that Aristotle's philosophical system contained many problematic elements from the point of view of Church doctrine, and many theologians were becoming increasingly nervous about the continued reliance on Aristotle for theological purposes.

The most significant bone of contention – from the point of view of the subsequent development of philosophy – was that Aristotle's metaphysics and physics assumed that the natural order contains features that cannot be otherwise. Aristotle, like all of the ancients, assumed that part of the business of natural philosophy is to identify those features of the natural order which are necessary. While there is much that is accidental and contingent in the world, these features of the natural order are not really intelligible. It is only those features of the natural order which cannot be otherwise – those obeying the principle of sufficient reason – which human beings can, at least in principle, come to understand. Now the Aristotelians thought that they had identified many such features of the natural order. Claims like 'There can be only one world' and 'The world cannot be moved with rectilinear motion' are good examples of ways in which Aristotelians thought the world has to be and ways the world cannot be. But such claims clash with the doctrine of divine omnipotence. The theologians had determined that the God of the Hebraic and Christians Bibles can do anything which is possible. And they maintained that the realm of the possible is limited by logic alone, and certainly not by Aristotelian metaphysics.

In 1277 these tensions came to a head when the bishop of Paris issued a list of condemned propositions, propositions that were not to be taught in universities on pain of excommunication. Effectively these condemnations stipulated that all portions of the ancient intellectual heritage that placed non-logical limits on divine omnipotence were no longer to be tolerated. The effect of this on philosophy and reason was devastating. Now it became impossible to say that a thesis about the natural order was true unless it was logically necessary and its falsehood logically impossible. This meant that philosophers now had to entertain the wildest ideas with all seriousness unless those ideas were logically incoherent. So while a philosopher could still safely ignore, say, the suggestion that a part was bigger than the whole of which it is a part, the philosopher could not rule out the possibility, say, that their visual experiences of things in world were actually caused by an evil demon bent on deceiving them, for there is no logical contradiction to be found in such a scenario. Here is the ultimate source of Hume's philosophical delirium.

The upshot of these condemnations was that severe limitations were placed on what reason and philosophy could establish with any confidence on any topic, and so it became impossible to believe that reason could ever establish anything of interest about matters of the faith. As Nicolas of Autrecourt lamented in the mid-1300s, if all philosophy has to go on is the principle of non-contradiction, then philosophy cannot establish the existence of the external world let alone cast light on the mysteries of the Trinity or the incarnation.[13] This had two consequences. Firstly, the scholastic project of synthesizing faith with reason was holed below the water line. Unaided Reason simply cannot penetrate Faith. Secondly, philosophers who heeded the condemnations now had to conduct their activities with only one sure principle, the principle of non-contradiction. Trying to overcome scepticism while relying on nothing more than this principle is essentially the Cartesian project as outlined in *The Discourse on Method* and practised in the *First* and *Second Meditations*. It is why Descartes was so attracted to the methods employed in geometry. In geometry axioms and definitions alone form the foundations of proofs for complex conclusions. Descartes hoped to employ the same methods in philosophy. But there would have been no motivation to do so if he had not been working within a post-1277 environment.

This leaves us with the rather ironic conclusions that Cartesianism was not born of Descartes, and that the father of modern philosophy was working within an environment shaped to its foundations by ultimately *theological* concerns. And this is not an insignificant historical aside. Much post-Cartesian philosophy bears the scars of facing up to the challenge of scepticism bequeathed to us from Descartes. Indeed most modern epistemologies and metaphysics have assumed precisely what the condemnations of 1277 insisted upon, namely, that there is no necessity except logical necessity. This assumption lies behind current understandings of the very nature of the philosophical enterprise, the rules according to which its business is to be conducted, and even some cherished inference patterns. We shall be looking at particular instances in the next chapter.[14]

Why was Descartes so successful in reshaping the self-image of philosophy? Why are the post-Cartesian philosophers that made it into the orthodox cannon of Western philosophy – the Spinozas and Leibnizs, the Lockes and Berkeleys, perhaps most importantly, the Malbranches and the Humes – precisely those who followed Descartes rather than those who remained true to Aristotle? This is a fascinating question, to which I have no definitive answer. But I would hazard to guess that the answer has less to do with the intrinsic merits of Cartesianism per se, and more to do with the 'spirit of the age' in Northern Europe following the Protestant Reformation. The Reformation in particular, and the general anti-Spanish/Hapsburg sentiment that was rife at the time, made Catholic and Spanish thinkers deeply suspect in the eyes of Northern Europeans. It is this same spirit which at least partly explains why a Hugo Grotius is a well-known if little read figure, while a Francisco de Vitoria is neither well-known nor read, despite both being groundbreakers in the field of international law. And it also goes some way to explaining why the myriad Church figures who played key roles in the development of numerous sciences have tended to be 'air-brushed' from popular accounts of the history of science.

But whatever the historical explanation for the success of Descartes's image of philosophy, the moral of this story as far as this work is concerned is that there is no need for the contemporary philosopher to accept the condemnations of 1277. After all, we are not Catholic theologians working under threat of excommunication. Nor are we Protestant theologians who need to worry either about the strength of the Spanish navy or about the Counter-Reformation. So there is no extra-philosophical pressure to accept that the only necessity is logical necessity, and so there is no need to build up a system of definitions, axioms and propositions in the quest for certainty, or to work assiduously to show that such a project can or cannot be made to work. We are free, that is, to return to the pre-Christian, Aristotelian idea that philosophy deals with aporia, dilemmas thrown up when we notice that lines of thought we are inclined to support appear to be contradictory. This was precisely the model of philosophy employed in Chapter 1 of this book where the project of synthesis is to be carried out on the various first-order sciences, between these and common sense, and between the various elements of one's social order. I recommended this model of philosophy there in order to bring philosophy into contact with the wider world.[15] In the next chapter I will focus on the techniques used by the scholastics in their attempts to come to terms with their aporia. Here too we have much to learn.

CHAPTER FOUR

Scholasticism on the various kinds of distinction

In the last chapter I set out the scholastic project of synthesizing Faith and Reason, religion and philosophy, Augustine and Aristotle. I presented this project as adopting Aristotle's aporetic method insofar as it deals with contradictions obtaining between otherwise plausible lines of thought. In this chapter I turn to the consideration of the classic scholastic methodological procedure: the drawing of distinctions. This chapter sets out Suarez's account of the scholastic understanding of the various kinds of distinction to be found in the real order. Familiarity with this material is, I argue, an essential element of any sound philosophical training. If being able to draw appropriate distinctions is a prerequisite of philosophical competence, then medieval philosophy matters.

> To be really the same excludes being really other, but does not exclude being other modally or mentally. (Suarez, *Metaphysical Disputations*, VII, 65)

Introduction

In *What Philosophers Know*, an excellent recent work on meta-philosophy, Gary Gutting sets out a case for the cultural significance of analytic philosophy. The basis of his claim is that 'there is a body of disciplinary philosophical knowledge achieved by ... analytical philosophers of the last fifty years'.[1] And not just any knowledge: 'This is a substantive body of knowledge and one of great cultural significance', he says; 'those without access to this knowledge will be severely limited in the essential reflective dimension of human existence.'[2]

Such an enthusiastic and positive assessment of philosophy's contribution to culture is rare these days. But Gutting carefully qualifies his claims. In particular, he insists that this philosophical knowledge does *not* amount to answers to the so-called 'Big Questions'. Rather this knowledge amounts to second-order knowledge about 'pictures' of philosophical projects and their viability, and about the role of intuitions or convictions in philosophical reflection. But that is not all:

> There is a substantial body of first-order philosophical knowledge – knowledge not about philosophical pictures but about the subject matter (language, necessity, knowledge, etc.) treated by those pictures. Such knowledge is typically about the nature of fundamental *distinctions* and the limits of their application. It is often ignored because it is not ordinarily the goal of philosophical reflection but a by-product of (generally unsuccessful) efforts to answer standard 'big questions'.[3]

In this chapter I want to build on Gutting's point about philosophy being a source of knowledge of distinctions to further my general case for scholasticism. To treat as the same things that are different, and to treat as different things that are the same, is to be confused, and this confusion inevitably leads to error. To avoid falling into this kind of confusion one needs to be able to recognize sameness and difference in the things we are thinking about. Key to this ability is a mastery of distinctions. This is why Gutting's claim regarding the significance of analytic philosophy has plausibility: *any* addition to our knowledge of fundamental distinctions constitutes a significant intellectual contribution.

Now the main claim of this chapter is that no one knew distinctions like the scholastics. Not only were they particularly adept at drawing important distinctions, they systematically drew important distinctions between distinctions. In fact, developing a comprehensive account of the various kinds of distinction became a topic of sustained study in its own right as scholastic practice became more and more sophisticated. As will become clear in the course of this chapter, these efforts to clarify the nature of distinctions were anything but a mere 'by-product' of work on other matters.

Unfortunately what these scholastic philosophers used to know about distinctions no longer forms a part of standard philosophical training. One can thumb through countless introductory textbooks and dictionaries of philosophy without encountering any mention of distinctions per se.[4] This is odd on the face of it. Philosophers are used to drawing distinctions in the course of our bread and butter activities, but we rarely stop to ask the follow-up question regarding the kind of the distinction we are drawing attention to. And, ironically, this is because we tend to treat distinctions as though they are all fundamentally the same, failing to recognize the differences between them. Often this is perfectly harmless. But in the right context, particularly when identity claims are at issue, this oversight leads to serious error. This is why being introduced to the various kinds of distinction is a fundamental part of a sound philosophical training. If distinctions matter, then scholasticism matters to all would-be philosophers.

I begin this chapter by focusing on the context in which the scholastic work on distinctions emerged. We can then consider the most developed account of this material we have, namely Suarez's *Metaphysical Disputations* VII, *On the Various Kinds of Distinction* (MD VII). This material in hand, we will then revisit some famous arguments from post-scholastic philosophers to illustrate the value of this training.

How to resolve contradictions

Recall that the scholastic project amounts to synthesizing the lines of thought present in the ancient heritage of Greece, Rome and the Hebraic religions of Judaism and Christianity. In the early days this meant confronting the contradictions to be found in this material. As this work became more and more self-conscious certain rules were formulated to guide this activity. For example, Abelard sets out some guidelines in his *Sic et Non*: a first priority was to gain a basic linguistic competence in Greek and Latin. If one finds two church fathers contradicting each other, for example, it might be that one has simply failed to understand what they were saying because one does not fully understand the language they were using. Second, before concluding that two authorities are contradicting each other one needs to make sure one is working with reliable texts. If texts have been corrupted because of repeated copy errors, or because the text has been physically degraded, or is incomplete with only fragments remaining, then one cannot be confident that the author's true views can be gleaned from them. Third, one must make sure not to attribute views to an author when they are merely reporting a view of someone else (easy to do if you are dealing with only fragments of a text). Fourth, one cannot ignore the context in which a text was written. It might very well be the case that an author has expressed a view on some topic or other, but that view was intended to apply only in the particular circumstances obtaining at the time of writing rather than being a claim of general or universal import. Fifth, one needs to consider the possibility that an author might use terminology that has changed in meaning over the centuries. Moreover, an author's use of terms might be idiosyncratic. The take-home message is that one must have a sophisticated understanding of an author's *oeuvre* before their communicative intentions can be confidently ascertained.

Now these guidelines really amount to rules of good scholarship. Nothing of particularly philosophical import has entered the picture as yet. But if one has observed all these guidelines and a contradiction remains unresolved, then one has to draw on other resources. One of the standard moves in a theological context is to distinguish between four different senses a piece of text can bear. There is the *literal* meaning of a text – a meaning identified with the help of observing the rules of good scholarship already noted – and then there is the *spiritual* meaning of the text. The spiritual meaning of a text arises from the fact that things and events in the world picked out by the literal meaning of the text can themselves have a meaning.[5] Spiritual meanings come in three main types: anagogical, moral and allegorical. The details of these different senses need not detain us here; it is sufficient to note that recognizing a distinction between the literal and the spiritual meaning that a text can bear affords a way of reconciling prima facie contradictory texts. For example, if one authority presents an account of God which implies that God does not have a material body, say, but a passage of the

Old Testament mentions God's hand, then one way out of the apparent contradiction might be to say that one passage is to be taken literally and the other non-literally. The phrase 'God's hand', for example, might simply be a non-literal way of referring to God's power without implying that God has a hand. Here we are starting to get into semantic theory, and so closer to issues of a recognizably philosophical nature. Indeed it is here that one finds the historical roots of philosophical hermeneutics, the study of the interpretations of texts.

Now, as we have seen, the drawing of distinctions has already entered the picture, but the distinctions mentioned so far have been distinctions in the realm of meanings. Another way to deal with contradictions between authorities is to appeal to distinctions in things themselves. If two authorities seem to be saying contradictory things about X, and all the previously mentioned manoeuvres have failed to remove the contradiction, it is still open to one to consider the possibility that X is *not* a fully unified, simple thing. It is true that one and the same thing X cannot be both Y and not Y. But if X were really a compound entity, that is, an entity with either distinct metaphysical components or integral parts, or a mereological sum of more than one entity (an aggregate), then it is open to one to consider the possibility that one authority is talking only about one aspect of X, say, while the other is talking about another aspect of X, with both claims able to be true simultaneously. If such a distinction in X proves plausible, then one would be able to accept the claims of both authorities because they are only prima facie contradictory. To develop this strategy scholastics make use of the Aristotelian metaphysics of unity and difference.[6]

Now this work really hits its stride under pressure to deal with (at least prima facie) contradictory claims about God. Many of the most pressing of these claims arise precisely because God was taken to be a simple entity – that is, an entity with no parts (metaphysical or integral)[7] – while still being the subject of distinct attributes like justice, wisdom or power. But this leads to a problem. If God is simple, then whatever *exists in* God *is* God. But if God's justice is God, and God's wisdom is God, how do we distinguish between the justice and wisdom of God? What do these terms mean when applied to God? And of course these difficulties were further amplified by the doctrine of the Trinity, according to which God not only has different attributes, but is three distinct persons in one. That is, the

Father, the Son and the Holy Ghost were each taken to be the same as the essence of God while not being the same as each other (for the Father is 'Unbegotten', the Son is 'Begotten' and the Holy Ghost is 'the procession'). This appears to flout the logical principle that things identical to a third thing must themselves be identical.[8]

One way out of these difficulties is to fall back on the strategy of drawing further distinctions within the realm of meanings. Aquinas, for example, claims that our knowledge of God is necessarily imperfect, God's nature being above human understanding. This epistemological point has implications for semantics. Our concepts and language are suited to cope with things within our epistemological range, but when these concepts and language are stretched to apply to things outside of our intellectual competence, there is semantic slippage. Terms in our language, 'wisdom' say, apply in one sense to creatures like human beings but in a different although related sense when applied to God. He writes,

> When any name expressing perfection is applied to a creature, it signifies that perfection as distinct from a man's essence, and distinct from his power and his being, and from all similar things. But when we apply 'wise' to God, we do not mean to signify anything distinct from his essence or power or being. And thus when this term 'wise' is applied to man, in some degree it circumscribes and comprehends the thing signified; whereas this is not the case when it is applied to God, but leaves the thing signified as uncomprehended and as exceeding the signification of the name. Hence it is evident that this term 'wise' is not applied in the same way to God and to man. The same applies to other terms. Hence no name is predicated univocally of God and of creatures. (*Summa Theologiae* I.I., q. 13, a. 5)

This is Aquinas's analogical theory of religious language. It draws on Aristotle's observation that a term like 'healthy' (his favourite example) can correctly be applied to diverse things like organisms, diets, lifestyles and urine samples, although the sense of 'healthy' is different in each case without being entirely equivocal.[9] This is an important point in the philosophy of language, and it has applications beyond theological concerns; but its primary application in theology is to provide 'wriggle room' when faced with prima facie contradictory claims about God.[10]

But not everyone was satisfied with the analogical approach to religious language. Scotus in particular maintained that if the terms of human languages can apply in a literal sense to creatures but only in a derivate and analogical sense to God, then it becomes impossible to have any natural knowledge of God because one will not be able to reason from truths about creatures to truths about God.[11] But Scotus insisted that it must be possible to apply terms *univocally* to God and creatures if the project of faith seeking understanding is to be viable. Thus he worked hard to show precisely this, that human beings, despite our cognitive limitations, are able to generate concepts that apply univocally to God and creatures.[12] Whether he was successful is not our concern here. The point for our present purposes is that if Scotus's general dissatisfaction with the doctrine of analogy is broadly correct, then the 'wriggle room' provided by Aquinas is removed. This takes us back to square one: how can God have distinct attributes while being simple? How can God be three distinct persons simultaneously? It is under this kind of pressure that the scholastics came to focus on the nature of distinctions *in things in the real order* rather than merely in meanings or senses.

But the broader point for us today is that philosophers can profit from these scholastic labours even in the absence of interest in the theological problems that gave rise to them. This material on the general kinds of distinctions proves to have applicability far beyond the original theological context because so many purely philosophical questions hang on sameness and difference claims. Indeed sameness and difference issues remain at the heart of much contemporary philosophical thinking in the form of debates regarding identity claims. We have already seen in our discussion of the problem of change that it amounts to explaining how *one and the same* thing can have *different* properties at different times. This is to explain how the same thing can be different from itself. And the problem of universals boils down to explaining how two numerically *distinct* things, Peter and Paul, say, can be *the same* in species. Consider also that in the philosophy of mind physicalists and substance dualists argue about whether minds are *distinct from* or *the same as* bodies. In meta-ethics naturalists and non-naturalists argue about whether moral facts are *distinct from* or *the same as* natural facts. And in metaphysics substantivalists and relationists argue about whether space is *distinct from* or *the same as* material bodies and their interrelations, while eternalists and presentists argue about whether time is *distinct from* or *the same as* change in material bodies. In each case one party argues for distinctness, while the other insists on identity or sameness. But much of this purely philosophical debate is conducted without a refined sense of the various kinds of distinction that might be at issue in each case. Just as a surgeon requires sharp tools, philosophers require sharp conceptual distinctions. But when our mastery of the concepts of sameness and difference is compared to that achieved by the scholastics, it becomes painfully clear that we have been operating with very blunt tools indeed.

What philosophers used to know

Most of the main figures in the scholastic tradition had important points to make about the nature of distinctions. But I will rely on Suarez for my account here because his MD VII summarizes over 300 years of work by his predecessors. Suarez has his own distinctive contribution to make, but his work is a veritable compendium of scholasticism, and virtually every major thinker is discussed before his own position is presented. It is therefore an invaluable source of scholastic lines of thought.

In *On the Various Kinds of Distinction* Suarez completes his study of unity and difference. MD V deals with numerical unity (what is it to be an individual), and MD VI deals with formal unity (what it is for Peter and Paul to be numerically distinct individuals while both being the same in species). In MD VII Suarez shifts his focus to consider the various ways in which things can be distinct.[13]

As Suarez points out, a full account of the various kinds of distinction is necessary if one is to have a complete account of unity. For there are as many ways of being unified as there are ways of being distinct. On this all were agreed; but there was considerable debate regarding the various kinds of distinction that should be recognized, and much dispute over their alleged instances. There was general agreement that many things in the real order are *really* distinct, in senses to be explored below, while some things are only *conceptually* or *mentally* distinct. But Duns Scotus upset the consensus by postulating a kind of distinction in things lying between fully real distinctions and merely conceptual distinctions.

It was debate over Scotus's so-called 'formal' or 'modal' distinction that led to sustained discussion of these matters culminating in Suarez's own efforts.

We can start with those distinctions that all accepted as having genuine instances, the three kinds of real distinction and the so-called 'mental distinction'. Real distinctions come in the following kinds:

- The *real essential* distinction: If *A* and *B* are not of the same natural kind, then they are essentially distinct.

This is the highest degree of distinction. To illustrate with an uncontroversial example, Peter is essentially distinct from a cabbage because neither has the nature of the other, Peter being a member of *Homo sapiens*, and cabbages being instances of *Brassica oleracea*. The other two kinds of real distinction are of greater intrinsic philosophical interest. These leave essences out of the reckoning and employ the principle that nothing can be separated from itself:

- The *major real* distinction: If *A* can exist in the real order without *B*, and *B* can exist in the real order without *A*, then there is a major real distinction between *A* and *B*. This *two-way* separation constitutes the kind of distinction we find between, say, two distinct human beings, Peter and Paul.

To this a further real distinction was added the following distinction:

- The *minor real* distinction: If *A* can exist in the real order without *B*, but *B* ceases to exist in the real order if separated from *A*, then there is a minor real distinction between *A* and *B*. This *one-way* separation is found between Peter and Peter's accidental properties such as his height and weight, his hair and eye colour, his spatial location or his actions.

Although weaker than two-way separation, this *one-way* separation was deemed sufficient to posit a real distinction between *A* and *B* because the distinction exists *ex natura rei*, or *a parte rei*, that is found in real things prior to any consideration by the mind. Unfortunately this distinction is sometimes referred to as a 'modal' distinction; but as Suarez reserves this term for a different distinction I will stick with his suggestion that we call one-way separation a minor real distinction.

It is worth mentioning a complication at this point. While the nature of the minor real distinction is clear enough, there was much debate over instances. It was assumed across the board that the accidents of a substance could not *naturally* continue to exist if separated from the substance in which they naturally inhere, and so there was at least a minor real distinction between a substance and its accidents. However, it was accepted by all that, by God's power, accidents could be preserved in the real order when separated from the substance in which they naturally inhere. This was accepted as established by the standard interpretation of the Eucharist, known as transubstantiation, according to which the properties of the host continue to exist although the underlying substance in which it naturally inheres has been altered. This example of God's omnipotence, insisted upon in the post-1277 environment, encouraged a tendency to consider accidents and properties as 'things' in their own right on a par with substances. As a consequence, some posited a major real distinction between a substance and its accidents. But however one takes the theology, allowing one-way separation to constitute a real distinction means that there is at least a *minor* real distinction between a substance and its properties.

The other kind of distinction widely recognized by the scholastics is the so-called 'conceptual' or 'mental' distinction:

- A *mental* distinction: If *A* and *B* are numerically identical in the real order, but we have two different ways of conceiving of *A* and *B*, then there is a mental distinction between *A* and *B*.

To use a familiar example, there is only a mental distinction between the Morning Star and the Evening Star since these are two names for numerically the same thing, that is, the planet Venus. It is important to recognize that a mental distinction is *not* a distinction between concepts, as one might distinguish between the concept 'dog' and the concept 'cat'. In fact there is a real distinction between these two concepts because each can be preserved without the other. A mental distinction is taken to be a distinction that we draw when thinking about things in the real order but which is not found in things themselves prior to our consideration of them. As Suarez says,

> This sort of distinction does not formally and actually intervene between the things designated as distinct, as they exist in

> themselves, but only as they exist in our ideas, from which they receive some denomination. (MD VII, p. 18)

The central point about this kind of distinction is that it is mind dependent:

> The properly so-called ... mental distinction of which we are speaking does not exist strictly by itself, but only dependently on the mind that conceives things in an imperfect, abstractive and confused manner, or inadequately. Since this distinction is not found in nature nor in the object known, it consists solely in a certain denomination issuing from concepts of the mind. (MD VII, p. 21)

Mental distinctions come in two types:

(a) Identity statements: When I say that *A* is identical to *B* my form of language suggests a relation between *A* and *B*, but *A* and *B* are not really but only mentally distinct.

(b) Identity statements based on inadequate concepts: An inadequate concept is one that does not capture 'the whole reality contained in the thing' either by being partial, or by being false, or by being an extrinsic denomination.[14]

Two important corollaries follow: firstly, God draws no conceptual or mental distinctions because all of God's concepts are adequate; secondly, if *A* and *B* are only conceptually or mentally distinct, then *A* and *B* are not separable in the real order because nothing can be separated from itself.

Now the kinds of distinctions canvassed so far were relatively uncontroversial in the sense that everyone accepted that there are genuine instances of these kinds of distinction. But debate arose regarding Scotus's claim that there is a further important kind of distinction that is less than fully real but more than merely conceptual. He called this a 'formal' or 'modal' distinction:

- A *formal* distinction: If *A* is not *B*, but *A* cannot exist in the real order without *B*, and *B* cannot exist in the real order without *A*, and *A* and *B* are both found *a parte rei*, or *ex natura rei*, then *A* and *B* are formally distinct.

Such a distinction might be suggested to exist between God's justice and God's wisdom. If so, one would be able to claim that God's justice and God's wisdom are formally distinct attributes of God without compromising God's simplicity. The other famous example of a formal distinction posited by Scotus lies between the formal unity of an individual *A* (Peter's humanity, say) and the individual unity of *A* (whatever it is that distinguishes Peter from other humans). This individuating feature of Peter is what Scotus called the *haecceitas* of Peter. The idea in this case is that Peter's humanity and Peter's haecceitas are distinct things in the real order, but only formally distinct, meaning that one cannot separate Peter's humanity from his haecceitas, or his haecceitas from his humanity.

Now Aquinas never used this kind of distinction, and Ockham denies that it has any genuine instances, with all alleged examples collapsing into mere mental distinctions;[15] but Suarez sides with Scotus in thinking that *some* distinction lying between the real and the mental needs to be recognized for some purposes. This he calls a 'modal' distinction:

- A *modal* distinction: If *A* is not *B*, and *A* is not a property of *B*, but *A* cannot exist without *B even by God's power*, then *A* is modally distinct from *B*.

Suarez provides the following example of a modal distinction based on the idea that natural light depends on the Sun. Suarez asks us to consider the relations obtaining between three things, the Sun, day light and the dependence of day light for its existence on the Sun. Now between the light itself and the Sun there is at least a *minor real* distinction, as in the natural course of things the light cannot continue to exist without the Sun, while presumably the Sun can continue to exist without the light emanating from it.[16] But if we grant God's omnipotence, we can say that there is a *major real* distinction between the light and the Sun because God could continue to preserve both in the absence of the other. But now consider the *mode* of day light, that is, its natural dependence on the Sun. According to Suarez, the natural *dependence* of day light on the Sun, while not being the light itself, or a property of the light, is not separable from the light even by God's power. One cannot have light's dependency, if you will, without the light itself. It follows then that the dependency of day light is not really distinct from the light, but nor is this dependency merely mentally distinct from day light, since this dependency has nothing to do with our conceptions of light but is found *a parte rei*.

Suarez suggests that we deem this dependency *modally* distinct from day light, recognizing that this is not adding any new entity to the real order. The inherence of *X* in *X* is not a real thing above and beyond *X* and *X*, and so inherence does not figure as an independent element of his ontology. So a mode, although it exists *a parte rei*, is not a fully real thing either, while not being just a creature of the mind. Suarez's point is that we need to recognize a distinction between entities on the one hand, and the *way* these entities hang together on the other. These ways or 'modes', while not entities in their own right, are features nonetheless of the real order. Indeed they constitute the 'order' to be found in the real, and tracking that order is what understanding amounts to.

How does one 'know' if a real distinction obtains between *A* and *B*?

Now it is one thing to have a set of distinctions in one's intellectual tool box; it is quite another to know which kind of distinction obtains in any particular case. And the most pressing cases to consider are those where a *real* distinction (major or minor) is being mooted, for positing a real distinction between *A* and *B* is ontologically inflationary, while positing a mere modal or mental distinction is ontologically deflationary. And since one should not posit entities without necessity, it follows that one should not posit a real distinction without necessity (MD VII, 46). In general Suarez follows the rule that one should always posit the weakest distinction between *A* and *B* consistent with the evidence. If one can deal with a case by positing only a mental distinction, this is to be preferred to positing a modal or a real distinction. Similarly, if a modal distinction will do, then one ought not to posit a real distinction between *A* and *B*.

So, when is one justified in positing the strongest of distinctions? The scholastic answer is very straightforward:

- If *A* and *B* are *capable of separate existence in nature*, then they are really distinct. If the separation in question is two-way, then we have a major real distinction (and possibly a real essential distinction). If the separation is only one-way, then we have a minor real distinction. If *A* and *B* are not separable in the real order then at best we have a modal distinction, and possibly only a conceptual distinction.

Of course this answer is useful only if we have an answer to the follow-up question: When does one know that *A* and *B* are indeed *capable* of separate existence in nature? It is here that perhaps the most significant divide between scholastic and post-Cartesian philosophy comes into view. The scholastic answer is as follows:

- *Actuality is our only guide to possibility in the real order.* One knows that it is possible to separate *A* and *B* in the real order if one knows that *A* and *B* have *actually* been separated or are *actually* separate in the real order.

This knowledge can be acquired naturally, as when one sees *A*s and *B*s going their separate ways. This allows one to conclude that *A*s and *B*s in general are separable, and that the next *A* and *B* pairing one encounters is similarly separable. But this knowledge of actuality can also be revealed, as in the case of the Eucharist. No one has naturally acquired the knowledge that properties can exist when separated from the substance in which they naturally inhere. But because transubstantiation was taken to occur every time communion is celebrated, the scholastics concluded that in general it is possible in the real order for properties to exist without the substance in which they naturally inhere. In both cases, however, *actuality* is the guide to possibility in the real order.

This scholastic dictum regarding modal epistemology raises an obvious question. 'When no separation has been effected either naturally or supernaturally, how can a real distinction be recognised?' (MD VII, p. 49), asks Suarez. And true to his scholastic roots, his answer is that some real distinctions will inevitably be hidden from us. He writes,

> A sure sign of a real distinction is hardly forthcoming when things are such that naturally they are always and necessarily found to be really united to one another, and have not thus far been separated by divine intervention. I do not deny that many things of this kind may be found to be really distinct. ... I am merely pointing out that we lack a universal sign for discerning such a distinction.' (MD VII, p. 55)

But in keeping with the other scholastic dictum – don't add distinctions without necessity – Suarez insists that we must refrain from positing real distinctions when our evidence from the actual course of events in the real order justifies only a modal or mental distinction.

Now, as a general rule, post-Cartesian philosophers do *not* follow these strict guidelines regarding real distinctions. As we shall see in the next section, post-Cartesian philosophers routinely posit *real* distinctions on grounds that would not be accepted by the scholastics. Very often these grounds are drawn from the realm of concepts and the order of ideas, as we find in cases of so-called 'conceivability arguments'. But Suarez will have none of this. What holds in the realm of concepts is no sure guide to the real order:

> To be the same in concept does not exclude being really distinct or other, because reason unifies in concept things that are really other, just as, on the contrary, it distinguishes in concept things that are really the same. (MD VII, 65)

What flies in the order of ideas and the imagination is no indication of how things are in the real order. *Pace* the assumptions of the early analytic tradition, conceptual analysis and logic alone are no guide to modal epistemology and metaphysics according to the scholastics.

Some modern cases

The divide between scholastics and post-Cartesian philosophers on matters regarding modal epistemology has its roots in the condemnations of 1277 when the omnipotence of God was so strongly insisted upon. The most significant philosophical consequence of God's omnipotence is that God cannot be constrained by his creation, and that the only limits on His power are the limits of logic. In effect God can do anything in the real order short of bringing about a logical contradiction. But the scholastics were not confident that they could always determine what is in fact logically possible. For one can only be sure that a proposition expresses a genuine logical possibility if one can be sure that one's concepts are adequate to things referred to in the proposition. But one's concepts are frequently inadequate in virtue of failing to capture 'the whole reality contained in the thing'. So the scholastics routinely say that *if* *X* is logically possible, *then* it is possible for God to bring *X* about in the real order; but we rarely know if *X* is logically possible because the adequacy of our concepts to real things is rarely beyond doubt. This means that *actuality* remains the epistemological touchstone even in the realm of logical possibility.

Not so for post-Cartesians. Descartes and his followers to the present day take *conceivability* to be a guide to logical possibility. This means that an *imagined* state of affairs is to be deemed possible in the real order as long as it contains no contradiction. We have then a much easier means of transitioning from the realm of logic and ideas to the real order itself: if it is conceivable, then it is possible in the real order. This opens up a new modal epistemology according to which actuality is no longer the sole guide to possibility in the real order. It also means that there is less need to worry about the various kinds of distinction, for now a mere distinction in concepts is sufficient to establish a real distinction in the order of things. According to this new philosophical mindset, logic, thought experiments and psychological facts about what is humanly imaginable are taken as guides to possibility in the real order. A quick look at some famous cases will illustrate the significance of this divide on modal epistemology as it applies to identity and difference claims.[17]

Descartes and the real distinction between mind and body

What better place to start our consideration of cases than with perhaps the most famous argument regarding real distinctions in the orthodox canon, namely, Descartes's argument for the real distinction between mind and body in *Meditation 6*? Descartes's stated goal is to show that mind and body are distinct *substances*. Since substances are ontologically independent entities, Descartes needs to show that there is a *major* real distinction, namely, *two-way* separation, between mind and body. One-way separation, sufficient for a minor real distinction, is not enough to establish Descartes's desired conclusion regarding the possibility of post-mortem existence for the mind or soul.

Descartes's argument proceeds in two stages. In the first stage Descartes claims that he clearly and distinctly perceives that mind and body are distinct, and that anything he so perceives to be distinct can be separated by God, however closely united they might be in the natural run of things. Notice that Descartes is trading on separability issues here, as we might expect from someone who has read Suarez. And notice as well that God's omnipotence is being appealed to in the course of this argument, something we are now used to having read Suarez ourselves. This is exactly what we would expect of a *theologian* working in the post-1277 environment. Notice, however, that the argument violates the scholastic dictum that actuality is the only guide to possibility in the real order. The only actuality Descartes appeals to at this stage is an actuality regarding what he can clearly and distinctly perceive. This is not the kind of actuality in the order of things that a scholastic would take to be relevant in the case of mind–body identity and distinctness claims.

The second stage of the argument is a collection of reasons for thinking that Descartes clearly and distinctly perceives minds and bodies to be distinct. Famously he offers three supporting arguments, all of which trade on Leibniz's law. Leibniz's law states that if *A* and *B* are identical, then anything true of *A* must be true of *B*, and vice versa. The supporting arguments are simply cases where Descartes draws attention to something he takes to be true of minds which is not true of bodies, and vice versa, thereby establishing that minds and bodies cannot be identical. The first two alleged instances, which trade on what Descartes believes he knows or can doubt about minds and bodies, can be ignored since Leibniz's law famously fails in intentional contexts. But the third supporting argument, which trades on the divisibility of bodies and the indivisibility of minds, does not fall at this hurdle. The claim here is that there is something which is true of bodies (they are divisible) which is not true of minds (they are indivisible). So by Leibniz's law minds and bodies cannot be identical. And because they are not identical, they must be distinct. And from this Descartes concludes that he has shown that there is a major real distinction between minds and bodies.

For the sake of argument let us waive concerns about whether Descartes is right with respect to the indivisibility of minds and the divisibility of bodies. What should someone familiar with the scholastic teaching on the various kinds of distinction make of this argument? The first point will be that the argument does indeed show that there is a distinction *of some kind* between minds and bodies. But it remains to be seen if the distinction in question is a major or minor real distinction, a modal distinction, a formal distinction or merely a mental distinction. At issue is whether Descartes has provided any reason to think the distinction is a major real distinction, as is required by substance dualism. Since it is a scholastic dictum never to posit a distinction stronger than is necessary to deal with the facts of the case in hand, at issue is whether one *must* posit a major real distinction to accommodate the fact that there is something true of bodies that is not true of minds. And the straight answer is 'No', for recognizing a minor real distinction is sufficient to accommodate this fact.

Consider the fact that substances have many properties that their accidents do not. For instance, my body weighs an undisclosed number of pounds, but the movements of my body do not weigh anything. Therefore, by Leibniz's law, my body and the movements of my body are distinct. But to anyone familiar with Suarez's work on the various kinds of distinction it is readily apparent that a minor real distinction is sufficient to accommodate these facts regarding weight, and that there is as yet no reason to think that my movements can be separated from my body with two-way separation. Similarly it is open to one to say that mental phenomena are the activity of the brain. What is true of the brain need not be true of the activity of the brain, so, by Leibniz's law, they are distinct; but there is no need to think they are capable of the two-way separation necessary to substance dualism. Descartes's mistake is born of the fact that he is insufficiently familiar with the various kinds of distinction that might obtain between minds and bodies, and unfamiliar with the signs of the major real distinction in particular. Or so the scholastic would say.

Chalmers's zombie argument: Minds are distinct from bodies

It is not just early modern philosophers who are guilty of this neglect of important distinctions. Another argument that has received its fair share of attention is Chalmers's version of the zombie argument which is simultaneously an attack on physicalism and a defence of substance dualism. Physicalism states that minds and mental phenomena are in some sense reducible or identical to, and certainly inseparable from, brains or states of brains. According to physicalism, minds are nothing over and above their causes in physical things. Chalmers, like Descartes, wants to show that physicalism is false, and this requires establishing that minds are distinct from bodies. And like Descartes, Chalmers has to establish that there is a *major real* distinction between minds and bodies if his substance dualism is to be of interest. This requires showing that there is two-way separation and not merely one-way separation between minds and bodies. To this end Chalmers offers the following argument:[18]

(1) We can conceive of a world which is physically identical to ours but which lacks features that ours has. In particular, we can imagine people (zombies) who are physically identical to us but who lack consciousness.

(2) Conceivability is a good guide to logical possibility.

(3) Zombies are logically possible (from (1) and (2)).

(4) We are not zombies, since we are conscious.

(5) There is a logically possible world which is a physical duplicate of the actual world while being mentally different (from (3) and (4)).

(6) Physicalism, that is, the view that a complete physical description of the world exhausts all that it contains, is false (from (5)).

Note that in the first premise separability does play a role in this argument for distinctness, although Chalmers neglects to specify whether this is one-way or two-way separation. This is an obvious deficiency in the argument since substance dualism requires two-way separability. But at a minimum we can take Chalmers to be saying that consciousness *can be* separated from human bodies. How do we know this? Well, if one is a scholastic, one can appeal to actuality and point out that in the case of a recently deceased human being one still has the brain (its anatomy is still intact) while consciousness is absent (the brain's physiological activities are no more). But note that this *actual* separation justifies only the positing of a minor real distinction between minds and bodies, and so will not allow one to draw the conclusion Chalmers seeks. But Chalmers is not a scholastic, and like many post-Cartesian philosophers he thinks that conceivability is a guide to possibility in the real order. So he answers our question differently, basing it on what is conceivable, not what is actual. But there is no legitimate move from what is merely conceivable to what is logically possible, and no straightforward move from logical possibility to actuality, unless one accepts that logical possibility is sufficient to establish possibility in the real order. But scholastics deny the first point, and secular philosophers have no right to the second. Chalmers does not even wave at a supporting argument for these crucial assumptions. This means that Premise (1), while possibly true, is of no use to Chalmers if he seeks to persuade a scholastic. But Premise (2) would be rejected, and so is similarly of no use. But even if Premises (1) and (2) are taken to imply that zombies are logically possible, no move has yet been made to establish anything about the real order. Premise (4) the scholastic can grant with equanimity. Premise (5) about logically possible worlds remains firmly fixed in the realm of concepts, revealing nothing about the real order. So the conclusion, that physicalism must be false, is a *non sequitur* and entirely unsupported. Chalmers betrays no awareness of what is required to establish a major real distinction, and comes nowhere near establishing his target conclusion. All this argument establishes, at best, is that it is logically possible that physicalism is false. But no physicalist need deny this.

Moore's ethical non-naturalism

Let us consider one more important case from the twentieth century: Moore's Open Question Argument against naturalism in meta-ethics. Historically this is a particularly important argument because it led, however unintentionally, to the rise of anti-realism in meta-ethics. And anti-realism in meta-ethics is in turn historically important because it is a major factor in the generation of the aporia outlined in Chapter 1 of this book. It is precisely because anti-realism was orthodoxy in the first three quarters of the twentieth century that it became mandatory to say that science, which deals with facts, could not speak to values, with values floating free of the realm of facts to become a subjective affair. How does this argument go, and what would a scholastic make of it? I follow Alex Miller's account of the argument here:

1. Suppose that the predicate 'good' is synonymous with, or analytically equivalent to, the naturalistic predicate '*N*'. Then,
2. It is part of the meaning of the claim that '*x* is *N*' that '*x* is good'. But then,
3. Someone who seriously asked 'Is an *x* which is *N* also good?' would betray some conceptual confusion. But,
4. Asking the question 'Is an *x* which is *N* also good?' betrays no conceptual confusion. Given any natural property *N* it is always an open question whether an *x* which is *N* is good. That is to say, it is always a significant question, of any *x* which is *N*, whether it is good. So,
5. It cannot be the case that 'good' is synonymous with, or analytically equivalent to, '*N*'. So,
6. The property of being good cannot as a matter of conceptual necessity be identical to the property of being *N*.[19]

The first thing to note is that the scholastic need have no quarrel with Premises (1)–(5). It is only with the move from the order of concepts to the real order, that is, the move from (5) to (6) that need give the scholastic pause. Moore's target conclusion is the claim that moral facts are non-natural, and his argument for this claim is that moral facts cannot be identical to natural facts. Since they are not identical to natural facts, the two kinds of facts must be distinct. Now, again, the scholastic will ask as to the nature of the distinction that Moore has established between moral and natural facts. And the answer is that Premises (1)–(5) establish at best a *mental* distinction between moral and natural facts, not the *major real* distinction he wants. And the reason for this claim has already been mooted:

> To be the same in concept does not exclude being really distinct or other, because reason unifies in concept things that are really other, just as, on the contrary, it distinguishes in concept things that are really the same. (Suarez, MD VII, p. 65)

Moore has shown that the term 'good' is not synonymous with any natural term '*N*'. So Moore has established that there is a difference in meaning between the term 'good' and any natural term one cares to choose. But does this establish that the referent of 'good' is not identical to the referent of any natural term '*N*' in the real order? The scholastic answer is an emphatic 'No'. The Morning Star and the Evening Star are mentally distinct, but Venus cannot be separated from itself in the real order. Their point is that noting a mere conceptual distinction is insufficient to establish a real distinction in things unless one assumes that the only necessity is logical necessity, and that our concepts are wholly adequate. But Moore offers no defence of either claim.

Like Descartes and Chalmers, Moore betrays no awareness of the various kinds of distinction to be found in the real order, or any familiarity with the signs of a major real distinction. But it would be very unfair to suggest that these three thinkers should be singled out as though they were unusually sloppy representatives of the philosophical profession. *Whenever identity and distinctness claims are made in post-Scholastic philosophy, they invariably betray a lack of sophistication, and a want of a basic philosophical training*. These kinds of distinctions and their signs were formally counted amongst the things that all philosophers know. They should be returned to the philosophical curriculum immediately. If mastering distinctions is a precondition of philosophical competency, then scholasticism matters to all would-be philosophers.

CHAPTER FIVE

The scholastics and arguments for the existence of God

Anyone arguing for the enduring philosophical value of scholasticism must counter the impression that the scholastics uncritically accept Catholic doctrine, and routinely rely upon invalid arguments for the existence of God. After some scene-setting, this chapter reconsiders an argument from Duns Scotus's little known masterpiece *De Primo Principio* alongside a more familiar offering from Aquinas. When properly understood, these prove to be cogent arguments for an ontologically basic entity, a conclusion that ought to attract the attention of metaphysicians. The rhetorical value of the chapter lies in showing that these scholastic arguments were anything but dogmatic, and anything but foolish.

Introduction

In the first three chapters of this book I tried to show (i) that philosophy as a discipline is not redundant, (ii) that a philosophical system able to do justice to common sense and the sciences is most likely to connect and find favour with those living outside the bubble of academe because it will be best placed to deal with current tensions in our social order and (iii) that the philosophical framework of the scholastics is precisely such a system. This is why medieval philosophy matters. In Chapters 4 and 5 I furthered this case by (iv) outlining the nature of the scholastic project of Faith seeking Understanding, and showing how that project mirrors the philosophical agenda outlined in Chapter 1, and (iv) showing how this project encouraged sustained work on the nature of distinctions, work with important implications for current philosophical debates. Much of this material will have been unfamiliar to anyone who is not a specialist in medieval philosophy. And I hope that these chapters might encourage some to look more closely at other scholastic contributions to first-order issues in metaphysics, logic, mind and ethics. But now, in this chapter, I need to address the elephant in the room, namely, what everyone thinks they already know about scholastic arguments for the existence of God.

God is a stumbling block to many in today's largely secular society. And one of the traditional barriers to medieval philosophy is the belief that the scholastics uncritically accepted obviously unsuccessful arguments for the existence of God. The charge is that the scholastics systematically compromised whatever philosophical loyalties they might have had to Aristotle in virtue of their having accepted the yoke of ecclesiastical authority, and that this is no more apparent than in their acceptance of various arguments for the existence of God. Now it is obvious that the scholastics took Church doctrine with the utmost seriousness. But I hope that the account of the scholastic project offered in Chapter 4 will have gone some way to countering the idea that the scholastics uncritically accepted Church authority. The point there was precisely the fact that the scholastic project is born out of a frank and explicit recognition of the contradictions to be found in the expressed views of authoritative figures. But the fact remains that anyone who would argue for the perennial interest and value of scholastic philosophy must find something sensible to say about the scholastic arguments for the existence of God. The primary burden of this chapter is to show that there is much good sense to be found in Aquinas's second way, and Scotus's 'coloured' version of the ontological argument.[1]

My main contention in this chapter is that the merits of scholastic arguments for the existence of God are rarely appreciated because they are so frequently misunderstood and misrepresented. Amongst the most common causes of this failure are as follows:

- **(i)** Assigning the arguments to the wrong domain
- **(ii)** Employment of inappropriate standards of argument evaluation
- **(iii)** An inadequate understanding of what 'naturalism' amounts to
- **(iv)** Misrepresentation of key claims within the arguments themselves

These arguments are so familiar that much scene-setting is needed if they are to be seen anew. So I will consider (i)–(iii) in some detail before looking at the arguments themselves. But the moral of the story is simple: when understood aright, the arguments to be discussed below provide philosophically respectable grounds for belief in an ontologically fundamental stratum of reality on which the existence of everything else depends. This ought to attract the attention of contemporary metaphysicians because, as we shall see, commitment to such an entity is not confined to the scholastics, but lies at the heart of most contemporary metaphysical systems.

Religion or metaphysics?

Before considering the details of Aquinas's second way, and the first stage of Scotus's *De Primo Principio*, a few preliminaries need to be addressed. If one is to learn anything from the scholastics it is vital that these arguments be approached with reasonable expectations. And perhaps the most important point to bear in mind in this respect is that these arguments have little or nothing to do with religion or the faith per se and everything to do with metaphysics. The arguments for the existence of God to be examined below are attempts to establish that a certain kind of entity exists, namely, an ontologically independent, necessary being on which all else depends. That is, the sole issue in these arguments – the issue that tends to get lost in the commentary – is whether there is an *ontologically fundamental entity* or 'level'. These arguments are not intended to establish anything more about this fundamental entity or level than this existence claim, and certainly nothing of religious significance.[2] Indeed most of what is taken to be religiously significant about God was deemed to be entirely beyond the remit of philosophical argumentation.[3] It is for this reason that these arguments are best seen as exercises in metaphysics, not the philosophy of religion or theology.

Recognizing that the burden of these arguments is to establish this narrow metaphysical point has important consequences. First, by taking the arguments out of the often inflammatory realm of religion and placing them in the intellectually dry and austere realm of metaphysics, I hope to calm the passions that often accompany discussions of these arguments, passions that dull or distort our critical faculties. Second, when these arguments are placed in the realm of metaphysics it becomes easier to notice that their conclusion is not nearly as exotic as one might have thought. Ironically enough, when God is *not* the focus of attention it is routinely assumed without much in the way of argument that there is an ontologically basic or fundamental entity or level. As Shaffer (2003) has shown, a commitment to an ontologically basic level is shared by Newtonian physicalists, Humean supervenience theorists, epiphenomenalists and atomists alike. Moreover, when these schools are challenged to defend this assumption their efforts are woefully inadequate. The points for our purposes though are, first, that the scholastic arguments for the existence of God are best seen as engaging in this *metaphysical* debate, a debate having very little if anything to do with religion per se and, second, that these arguments for the existence of God, if sound, would fill a lacuna in world views often thought to be diametrically at odds with those of scholasticism. In any case, we need to take some time to familiarize ourselves with this debate if we are to understand these arguments aright.

Is there an ontologically fundamental level?

As Shaffer has recently pointed out, contemporary metaphysics, along with the sciences, is animated by a shared view of reality with three key ingredients:

- **(a)** Reality is hierarchical, being stratified into levels.
- **(b)** There is a level of reality upon which all else depends (the ontologically fundamental level).
- **(c)** This fundamental level is most fully real, all else being ontologically derivative.

The common positions today, Newtonian microphysicalism, Humean supervenience, atomism and epiphenomenalism, all accept (b); they simply disagree as to the nature of that level. Microphysicalists maintain that this level is whatever a completed physics says the smallest particles or strings (or what have you) are; Humeans might say it is qualities of regions of space–time; atomists cling to indivisible atoms; and epiphenomenalists say it is where all the causal powers present in the world emanate from – whatever that might be.

But there are respectable people who reject (b). Leibniz, David Bohm and Shaffer himself are happy to sign up to 'the qualitative infinity of nature', 'the inexhaustible *depth* in the properties and qualities of matter', and to a reality with 'an infinity of levels'.[4] So we need to ask: are there good arguments for (b)? Shaffer says there are no good a priori arguments for (b), and as good naturalists, we should accept that this could not fail to be the case. More important is Shaffer's claim that the best a posteriori argument for (b) is extremely weak. That argument goes as follows:

1. There will be a completed microphysics (eventually).
2. It will postulate basic particles.
3. These particles will be that out of which everything else is composed.

Shaffer thinks there is no reason to take any of 1–3 seriously. We need not dally over these claims. The point for our purposes is that *this* is the debate in which the arguments for God need to be situated. And in *this* debate the scholastics feature on the side of Newton and company, not as foes. Moreover, Shaffer is right to claim that the four contemporary non-theistic schools have not done a very good job of showing why there could not be an *infinite* number of ontological levels, with no level enjoying a privileged ontological status. But what Shaffer does not do, as I think we should, is consider the arguments against the possibility of an infinite number of ontological levels to be found in the scholastic arguments for the existence of God, for this is precisely what these arguments are meant to establish. That Shaffer does *not* consider these arguments is not surprising because most commentators fail to understand the nature of the infinite regresses these arguments are seeking to rule out.

What standards of evaluation should we employ?

Another way in which expectations must be managed is with regard to the standards used in the evaluation of such arguments. It is a common human failing to employ double standards in the evaluation of evidence. We tend to employ exacting standards when dealing with evidence for conclusions we do not welcome, and more relaxed standards in cases of evidence for conclusions we already accept or would like to accept. In fact the scholastics are charged with precisely this failing inasmuch as it is alleged that they were inclined to accept dubious arguments for the existence of God because they had already accepted the conclusion as a matter of faith. But times have changed. Now it is critics of these arguments who are often guilty of insisting on standards of cogency when discussing arguments for the existence of God that one would not dream of employing in other quarters. It is for this reason that a preliminary discussion regarding standards of argument evaluation is necessary if we are to avoid the premature and unjust rejection of perfectly respectable arguments for the existence of God. To illustrate the problem of double standards it is worth considering in some detail a recent prominent publication on medieval philosophy of religion by Graham Oppy. Oppy serves as a paradigmatic example of double standards, but he is in no way alone in this respect.

In *The Oxford Handbook of Medieval Philosophy* Oppy (2012) presents the standards he suggests that arguments for the existence of God must meet if they are to be deemed 'cogent'. Oppy's contribution in this regard is particularly welcome if only because it makes explicit what is often left implicit. He begins his piece with the following unequivocal claim: 'We cannot learn how to prove the existence of God from medieval arguments for the existence of God' because none of the scholastic arguments is so much as 'cogent'.[5] The basis for *this* assertion is worth our close attention. None of the traditional arguments, nor the modified versions thereof, is 'cogent' because 'they are not plausible *demonstrations* that naturalism is *incoherent*'.[6] We will consider in the next section just what naturalism amounts to. But we can already see that Oppy's claim is quite remarkable. If Oppy were right, an argument for the existence of God would not be cogent if it merely gave good reasons to believe that there is an ontologically fundamental entity. Nor would it be cogent if it provided merely *probable* grounds for thinking that naturalism is *false*. According to Oppy, a cogent argument for God has to demonstrate that naturalism is, not just false but incoherent, that is, logically impossible. This is an unusually high bar that Oppy has set for medieval arguments for the existence of God.

Why is the bar for cogency set so high? Oppy says that any 'cogent' argument 'ought to convince anyone who does not already accept the conclusion to embrace the conclusion'.[7] And in the case of arguments for the existence of God the person to be convinced, says Oppy, is the agnostic. And to convince the agnostic, says Oppy, the argument must 'rule out' world views that deny the existence of God. And in order to achieve this, the argument must show that the assumptions underpinning those world views are incoherent. Since the key assumption of these world views is naturalism, any cogent argument for the existence of God must demonstrate the incoherence of naturalism.

Now there is much that is questionable about Oppy's standards of cogency. Firstly, if Oppy is to be believed, a 'cogent' argument for the existence of God has to be so strong as to rule out atheism and agnosticism on grounds of incoherence. But this means that, for all intents and purposes, a 'cogent' argument must be a 'knock-down' argument. But it is a common place that there are no 'knock-down' arguments in philosophy. As Quine – a naturalist himself – was wont to point out, *any* claim, however implausible it may be, can be retained if one is willing to make sufficient adjustments to one's belief set. Argument evaluation is ultimately a matter of professional judgement of the costs and benefits of accepting the conclusion of an argument. Often a good philosophical argument is one which brings to light the advantages or difficulties inherent in maintaining a given position, advantages or difficulties that may not have been obvious before the argument was proffered. There is no expectation of knock-down arguments here.

But perhaps the most important problem with Oppy's standards of argument evaluation is that they have little to do with the intrinsic properties of arguments themselves, and have everything to do with the argument's effectiveness in bringing about a psychological change in some person reflecting upon it. An argument for the existence of God is cogent, says Oppy, if it convinces the agnostic. But this is to put the cart before the horse: the psychological states of those contemplating an argument do *not* measure the argument; rather, the psychological states of those contemplating the argument are measured by the intrinsic merits of the arguments themselves. The vagaries of human psychology being what they are, there is any number of reasons why someone might be convinced, or fail to be convinced by an argument, reasons that may have little to do with the merits of the argument itself. So it is normal practice for logicians to focus on the intrinsic properties of arguments, isolating those properties that objectively establish the intended conclusion, regardless of whether anyone is actually convinced by them or not. To do otherwise is to wander into the sphere of rhetoric and to leave the domain of strict argument evaluation behind.

So what are the standards that one ought to insist upon when evaluating any argument, including arguments for the existence of God? Obviously it is important to insure that these standards are not cut to suit the rhetorical needs of the moment, so I offer here two independent voices on standards of argument evaluation, both gleaned from contexts having nothing to do with arguments for the existence of God. The first source is Mark Vorobej's *A Theory of Argument*. According to Vorobej, 'A cogent argument ... is an argument by which you ought to be persuaded.'[8] And an argument is 'cogent' for someone when they have reason to believe that an argument meets the following four conditions:

1. Each premise of the argument is true.
2. The set of premises is relevant to the argument's conclusion.
3. The set of premises grounds the conclusion.
4. Each premise plays a role in grounding the conclusion.[9]

Note that Vorobej's position is that one *ought* to be persuaded by arguments that meet these cogency conditions, not that an argument is cogent if one actually is persuaded by it. Note also that the cogency of an argument has nothing to do with properties of those contemplating it.

The same general position is to be found in chapter 7 of Hamblin's *Fallacies*.[10] On Hamblin's analysis a good argument must have the following features:

1 True premises.
2 A conclusion implied by the premises (via a valid form or some acceptable inference pattern).
3 The conclusion must follow reasonably immediately (no problematic gaps between premises and conclusion).
4 If some of the premises are unstated they must be of an omissible kind.

Again we have here a set of purely objective standards that all good arguments must meet, all being entirely independent of the perlocutionary effects such an argument might have on those contemplating it. Now, of course, we often deploy arguments to persuade others of a conclusion, and in such cases the truth of the premises, if unknown, will be of little value. So we might follow Hamblin and introduce a modified set of standards, as follows:

1 The premises must be known to be true.
2 The conclusion must follow clearly from the premises.
3 Unstated premises must be such as to be taken for granted by all concerned (as well as true).
4 The conclusion must be such that, in the absence of the argument, it would be in doubt.

Of course, this is still a rather high bar to clear, particularly when the premises are of an empirical nature where probability is the best we can hope for. In such cases we might be inclined to introduce a further modified set of standards as follows:

1 The premises must be reasonably probable.
2 The conclusion must follow clearly from the premises.
3 Unstated premises must be such as to be taken for granted by all concerned (as well as true).
4 The conclusion must be less probable a priori that the premises.

But, in the philosophical sphere, we are usually forced to recognize that our premises have not been established by any empirical studies, and cannot be handled using the methods of statistics, and yet we still feel that the premises have some claim on us. As Hamblin points out, such arguments tend to rely on 'intuitions', or common sense, or beliefs that have some standing in our intellectual community because they are thought to be implied or assumed by successful scientific theories. In such cases we are obliged to weaken the standards of argument evaluation still further. And we are likely to arrive at something like the following:

1. The premises must be accepted by reasonable people.
2. The passage from premises to conclusion must be of an accepted kind.
3. Unstated premises must be of a kind that are accepted as omissible.
4. The conclusion must be such that, in the absence of the argument, it would not be accepted.

I would submit that arguments that meet *any* of these sets of standards are cogent and non-defective. In logic classes we insist on Hamblin's first set, which makes no mention of the mental states of those contemplating them. In actual practice we tend to employ the final set. The last three sets do bring in reference to the mental states of those contemplating the argument, but they do not privilege the mental states of those who oppose the conclusion. None implies that there can be no cogent arguments for contrary conclusions. I would submit that as long as the arguments for the existence of God can meet at least one of this set of standards then they too are cogent and thus worthy of consideration. To ask for more is to be guilty of double standards.

Two naturalisms

Finally, a further barrier to appreciating scholastic arguments is that they are embedded in a metaphysical framework that is alien to most contemporary philosophers. The result is that often they are given short shrift simply because the contemporary reader does not share these background commitments. Very often the commitments in question are those associated with what is often called 'naturalism'. The common charge is that twenty-first century thinkers insist on a naturalist metaphysical framework, whereas the scholastics are happy to entertain thoughts of the supernatural. Now there are two points to be made here: firstly, it is often assumed that contemporary metaphysical systems are better than those of the scholastics, but this is seldom argued for explicitly. My hope is that previous chapters will have gone some way to showing that contemporaries have no right to this assumption. Secondly, and perhaps more surprisingly, it is far from obvious that the naturalism that animates contemporary metaphysics is on a firmer footing than the naturalism to be found in the Aristotelian-scholastic framework. So a comparison of naturalisms is in order before looking at the key claims in the arguments themselves.

A commitment to naturalism is usually taken to imply a respect for the sciences and the causal closure of the natural order. The root idea is that the scholastic arguments for the existence of God are unacceptable because they violate these naturalistic principles. Of course such criticism is only as strong as the claims of naturalism. But what naturalism amounts to has become a hotly disputed topic in recent years, so no casual appeal to naturalism should be allowed to go unchallenged. In this section I offer a detailed comparison of two 'naturalisms', one Quinean, the other neo-Aristotelian. The point of the comparison is twofold. The first is simply expository: I want to set out explicitly what 'naturalism' has been taken to mean. Secondly, I want to suggest that neo-Aristotelian naturalism is not obviously inferior to the Quinean version. Space considerations make it impossible to consider this topic as fully as it deserves. I confine myself here to charting the two positions, with expository comments kept to a minimum. Again, to avoid the appearance of bias, I take the account of Quinean naturalism from an independent source, and define neo-Aristotelian naturalism by its acceptance or rejection of the elements of Quinean naturalism.[11]

Principles of naturalism

Quinean	Neo-Aristotelian
Semantic holism: Individual statements have no empirical content.	*Reject.* There is nothing in Aristotelian semantic theory that forces semantic holism.
Confirmation holism: The Duhem thesis.	*Agree.*
Inclusion: Any system of beliefs with empirical content includes those which provide organization or structure to that system (no analytic/synthetic distinction).	*Indifference.* Aristotle and the scholastics accept the analytic/synthetic distinction, but they do not take it to be particularly significant, so denying it leaves no central doctrine in jeopardy.
Diffusion: Any belief which is part of a system with empirical content shares in the confirmation or disconfirmation that accrues to that system (no analytic/synthetic distinction).	*Agree.*
Methodological monism: Scientific method is the only method for all types of inquiry (i.e. Quineans reject Carnap's view that the methods of philosophy and science are distinct).	*Rejection.* Scholastics *reject* the thesis that the methods of philosophy are those of the sciences. Philosophy is *not* 'just more science'. However, scholastics reject Carnap's account of philosophical method as confined to conceptual analysis and exposition.
Continuity: Metaphysics is continuous with the sciences in the sense that both are subject to experiential checks.	*Agree.*
Anti-a priorism: There are no a priori beliefs of any kind.[12]	*Agree* if 'a priori' is taken in the modern sense, but not if taken in the original scholastic senses. Reasoning from causes to effects (i.e. reasoning a priori) and reasoning from effects to causes (i.e. reasoning a posteriori) are *both* perfectly respectable.

Quinean	Neo-Aristotelian
Anti-foundationalism: Justification does not have a foundationalist structure.	*Qualified agreement.* Justification of basic principles is dialectical. However, in a completed science its explanatory efforts will be foundationalist as per the *posterior analytics*.
Inheritance: The philosopher begins her thinking within the inherited world theory as a going concern (Neurath's image).	*Agree.*
Deference to scientific findings: Philosophy should defer to science. Its theories need to be consistent with the sciences.	*Qualified agreement.* Philosophy should defer to the sciences when the mature sciences are in agreement. So deference to science *as a whole*, but not necessarily to particular sciences in isolation. The reason for this is the presence of aporia arising from within the first-order sciences. Moreover, no hierarchy within the sciences is accepted by the neo-Aristotelian, unlike the Quinean who tends to privilege physics.
Deference to scientific method: Philosophy should only employ scientific methods.	*Rejection.* The empirically based methods of the sciences are not appropriate to aporia resolution.
Anti-supernaturalism: Supernatural entities, and cognitive faculties not consistent with evolutionary history of cognition, are to be rejected.	*Partial agreement.* No theoretical entity of any sort is ruled *in or out* prior to metaphysical reflection on aporia arising out of the sciences. Nonetheless, no cognitive faculties are allowed which are inconsistent with evolutionary theory.

(Continued)

Quinean	Neo-Aristotelian
Quantificational approach to ontology: (a) First, determine which scientific theories are the best available; (b) then translate the sentences of these theories into the language of first-order predicate logic. Determine one's ontology by reference to the quantifier: whatever is ineliminable from those sentences, and whatever is 'quantified over', is given a place in one's ontology.	*Reject:* (a) It is not the business of metaphysicians to determine what the best scientific theories are. That is the business of science. Metaphysicians accept what the sciences deem to be their best efforts to date as their starting point. (b) The paraphrase technique is rejected on the grounds that modern first-order predicate logic is metaphysically loaded. It is appropriate to mathematics but not to the natural order beyond its quantifiable aspects. (c) The appropriate ontological approach is the aporetic method.
Metaphysics is ontology: Metaphysics is the business of determining what there is.	*Qualified agreement:* Metaphysics includes ontology but is not confined to ontology. It is also, and perhaps most importantly, in the business of examining how the entities in the various ontological categories 'hang together' as an ontological system. Its point is also missing: metaphysics is to be engaged in in order to overcome aporia arising from the sciences in pursuit of the best overall theory.
Humean on causality[13]	*Rejection*: as we say in Chapter 2, neo-Aristotelians are causal realists, granting house room to efficient, material and formal causes, with some still holding out for final causes as well when appropriately construed.

Assignment 2 reading.

Now I hope this will g[illegible] ha[illegible] been taken to mean, as w[illegible] a[illegible] how much of this natu[illegible] scholastic can accept. I [illegible] it [illegible] readers to consider the details [illegible] arguments for the existence of God with these naturalisms in [illegible] to determine for themselves whether they fall foul of natu[illegible] not. But one point is worth emphasizing. The scholastic does not rule in or out any kind of entity prior to metaphysical reflection, including supernatural entities (whatever that might mean). This *does* violate the Quinean stricture against supernatural entities, but refusing to foreclose on the very possibility of a supernatural order is entirely consistent with *other* Quinean principles, namely, the rejection of the a priori, confirmation holism, diffusion and the continuity thesis. So there is an internal contradiction in the Quinean version of naturalism vis-à-vis supernatural entities. But on one point all naturalists can agree: all *philosophically* respectable beliefs have to be consistent with mature scientific theory, and they need to be the product of 'unaided' processes of cognition natural to *Homo sapiens*. Aquinas, for one, would happily accept this principle. So should we.

The cosmological argument: Aquinas's second way

With these extensive preliminaries out of the way, we can finally turn to the arguments themselves. I will focus on the so-called 'cosmological argument' (Aquinas's second way) and a version of the ontological argument because these are likely to be at least somewhat familiar to readers of all backgrounds. I will not discuss these arguments in full because there are innumerable accounts presented in standard anthologies of philosophy of religion. Nor will I discuss all the various criticisms to be found in the literature. The reason why this is not entirely remiss of me is that many discussions of these arguments fail to represent them accurately, and so many criticisms simply miss their mark. Moreover, with regard to the cosmological argument I will confine myself to a discussion of the crucial premise regarding the impossibility of an infinite series of causes. Everything depends on how this premise is understood.

The argumentative strategy of Aquinas's second way can be stated as follows:

1 Nothing can cause itself to be.

Self-causation is ruled out because it involves the contradiction of existing (in order to be a cause) and not existing (in order to be brought into existence) at the same time. So,

2 If something begins to be, its existence is caused by something else.
3 Now either (i) there is an infinite series of such things caused to be by other things that are themselves caused to be, or (ii) there is something which causes other things to be but is not itself caused to be by any other thing.
4 (i) is impossible, so
5 There is something which causes other things to be but is not itself caused to be by any other thing. This is what it is to be an ontologically basic entity.

Waiving objections based on the possibility of something spontaneously coming to be (which undercuts the very intelligibility of reality) and those which suggest the possibility of a causal loop, with the causal series turning back on itself (which involves a form of self-causation) our focus centres on Premise 4. How is it to be understood, and why did the scholastics believe it?

Some important points for the proper understanding of this premise are necessary. Firstly, the scholastics say that infinite regresses of causes of a particular type are impossible in the material, formal and final causal orders as well as in the efficient order. It is particularly important to recognize that scholastics rule out infinite regresses of internal causes (material and formal) just as much as infinite regresses of extrinsic efficient and final causes because, as we shall see in a moment, this is what links these arguments to the concerns of Shaffer.[14]

A second vital point is that *some* infinite causal regresses *are* possible according to the scholastics. According to Aquinas one might very well be able to have infinite regresses of *accidentally ordered* causes. What everyone rules out, however, are infinite regresses of *essentially ordered* causes.[15] In accidentally ordered causal series the causal power of each of the causes in the series is independent of the causal activity of prior causes in the series. A standard example of such a series is the order of generations of human beings. My being able to generate offspring is independent of the causal powers of my parents inasmuch as I can still have the power to produce offspring even if my parents, let along my grandparents and great-grandparents, are no longer with us. Now according to Aquinas the order of generations is potentially infinite.[16] This is particularly important because what Aquinas is seeking to rule out is *not* an infinite past, where one generation gives way to another ad infinitum, but a different causal order altogether.

What Aquinas has an issue with is an infinite series of *essentially ordered* causes. In such a series the causal power of any cause in the series depends upon all prior causes in the series exercising their causal powers concurrently. Aquinas provides a mundane example himself. When I use my hand to move a stick, which moves a stone, which moves a leaf next to it and so forth, the causal power of the stick on the stone, and the stone on the leaf, depend on the concurrent causality of my hand. Remove the hand and the stick no longer moves the stone. A more philosophically interesting example of an essentially ordered causal series, relying on internal causes rather than external causes, is that found in the commitment to reality being stratified into levels. Consider your current mental states. Each of these depends upon brain activity. And this brain activity (physiology) depends upon brain tissues (anatomy), which in turn depend upon cells, which depend upon organelles, which depend upon large molecules, which depend upon atoms of the various elements, which depend upon protons, neutrons and electrons and so forth. Remove any of these levels and everything above is lost. For the key point about essentially ordered causal series is that *all links in the causal chain must exist simultaneously*. Recognizing this point is crucial to understanding Aquinas's second way. For when Aquinas argues that there must be a first cause he is *not* talking of some event in the remote past[17]; Aquinas's first cause continues to be active at this very moment, God being the creator and *sustainer* of the world. We can make the point metaphorically as follows: the infinite causal series to be ruled out is *not* an accidentally ordered causal series working horizontally, as it were, across times, but an essentially ordered causal series operating vertically at an instant between concurrent hierarchically ordered levels of reality.

So why is an infinity of essentially ordered causes impossible? It is here that critics of the argument have seen their chance. And not without reason (although they usually target the wrong causal series). For the scholastics often offer here considerations that fail to convince. Yandell (2005, p. 190) nicely illustrates the problem. He presents an argument from Aquinas which goes as follows.

A causal series cannot be infinite because of the following:

1. An infinite series has no first member.
2. If a series has no first member, it has no later or succeeding members.
3. If a series has no first or succeeding members, then it has no members.
4. But no series can have no members. So
5. No causal series can be infinite.

But Yandell finds this argument 'puzzling' and cannot see why the distinction between accidentally and essentially ordered causal series, so carefully drawn by Aquinas, is at all germane to the issue. But this is because an important point of metaphysics has been missed.

It is true that the scholastics often give arguments denying the possibility of infinite regresses that fail to convince. But they usually do so after saying something like 'And no philosopher accepts such things' without explaining in detail why no philosophers accept such things. But the reason they provide no explanation is because it was perfectly obvious to them why philosophers rule out such things: they involve *a kind of category mistake*, that is, the predication of a property to an entity that is not apt to receive properties of that category.[18] The categories in question here are those of the actual and the possible, and the predicates are 'finite' and 'infinite'.

To see the difficulty one must begin by recognizing that the infinite is by definition indeterminate and indefinite because the infinite by definition lacks boundaries or an end. But actual beings, according to Aristotle, are always definite and determinately circumscribed. We must remember that, for Aristotle, the principles of bivalence and non-contradiction are primarily principles of metaphysics, not logic. That is, these principles apply to entities in the real order first and to propositions in the rational order second. And the reason these principles apply to entities of the real order is because actually existing things are always in some definite configuration. There are no vague things in Aristotle's world. Being determinate and definite is simply part of what it is to be actual for Aristotle.[19]

By contrast, being vague, indeterminate and indefinite characterizes *possible* beings. To see this consider your properties and those of your future great-great grandchild. You are actual, while your great-great grandchild is merely possible. You, being actual, are quite determinately circumscribed, and so the principles of bivalence and non-contradiction apply to you. Setting aside concerns having to do with the accuracy of our measuring devises, we can safely say of you that you are either 6 feet tall or not 6 feet tall (principle of bivalence), and that you cannot be 6 feet tall and not 6 feet tall at the same time and in the same respect (principle of non-contradiction). But the same cannot be said of the height of your future great-great grandchild, because this child has no actual properties by which to render them determinate. There is an ontological gap in the case of possible beings which undercuts the application of these principles. Indeed to be reduced from potency to actuality is largely a matter of becoming a definite, determinately circumscribed entity to which these principles of logic now apply. But the point for our present purposes is that the scholastics standardly work with a contrast between the actual and the possible as follows:

Actual being	Possible being
Definite	Indefinite
Determinate	Indeterminate
Specific	Unspecific
Finite	Infinite

This is why the distinction between accidentally and essentially ordered causes is crucial. In an essentially ordered causal series all the causes must exist simultaneously; that is, they must all be actual at the same time. This is not the case with an accidentally ordered causal series which exists only potentially. So if one were to have an infinite essentially ordered causal series, one would have an actual infinity. But this is to render definite that which is essentially indefinite, which is simply a conceptual confusion.[20]

The moral of this story is that there can be potential, that is, possible infinities (like the series of generations, where not all of the generations exist simultaneously), but there cannot be actual infinities in the real order (where an infinity of ordered levels exists simultaneously) because that would mean that something actual, and so definite, determinate and specific, is indefinite, indeterminate and vague. So there has to be an ontologically fundamental level to reality on pain of reality being indeterminate. This is the argument for Premise 4 which few commentators realize there is in the scholastics. It does *not* fall to the usual complaints brought against Aquinas's second way regarding infinite regresses. Nor does it violate any principles of naturalism.

Scotus's version of the ontological argument

The other famous argument for the existence of God is, of course, Anselm's so-called 'ontological argument'. As is well known, it has been the whipping boy of philosophers for centuries. What is less well known is that Aquinas and other scholastics were fully aware of the issues plaguing Anselm's version of the Ontological Argument.[21] They did not need to be enlightened by a Kant or a Quine on the nature of the concept of existence to see that the move from that which exists *in apprehensione intellectus* to that which exists *in rerum natura* is illicit without there being some acceptable transition enabler between the realm of ideas and the realm of real things. Aquinas thought that the only such enabler was empirical observation, and so his focus was on the so-called 'cosmological arguments'. Scotus followed Aquinas in favouring such arguments, but he thought another transition mechanism was worth exploring. This mechanism is the modal concept of possibility. His suggestion is that we can 'colour' Anselm's argument by showing that God is at the very least a possible entity inasmuch as there is nothing in the concept of 'God' which is incompatible with Being as such. From this mere possibility Scotus thinks he can establish the necessary existence of God. The argument proceeds as follows:

1 If God is possible in the real order, then God is actual in the real order.

2 God is possible in the real order. Therefore
3 God is actual in the real order.

Now Premise 1 had been forwarded by Avicenna, and for reasons to be considered in a moment, Scotus thinks this consequence holds. The challenge as he sees it is to establish Premise 2.

Now if Scotus accepted modern views on modal metaphysics securing the second premise would be relatively straightforward. *We* usually take something to be possible if *X* is conceivable; and we deem *X* to be conceivable if positing *X* leads to no *logical* contradictions. That is, we tend to take *logical* possibility and *conceivability by us* to be enough to establish *metaphysical* possibility. But as we saw in the previous chapter on distinctions, such an inference pattern is unavailable to the scholastics. The fact that the concept 'God' appears to be thinkable without contradiction is insufficient to establish that God is a possible entity in the real order. For Scotus, and for the scholastics generally, the only sure guide to what is possible in the real order is actuality in the real order. So to secure the second premise Scotus must argue from what we know to be actual in the real order to God's possibility in the real order. And to do this Scotus modifies Aquinas's second way. That is, Scotus argues from the *actual* dependence of things in the real order on a cause for their existence, to the possibility of God. That is, he argues that some things *can* be brought into existence by something else because, as Aquinas noted, some things *actually are* brought into existence by something else. Scotus then runs Aquinas's argument with the intention of taking it to establish that there *can* be a first cause in the real order. There *could* be such an entity, he says, because such an entity appears to be required to explain what we know is *actually* the case. This is the strategy for securing his second premise.

This modified version of Aquinas's second way has an interesting twist. As we saw in the case of Aquinas, explaining why an infinite regress of essentially ordered causes is impossible was the main burden he had to face. A similar challenge faces Scotus. But since Scotus is seeking merely to establish the possibility of God, he has room to manoeuvre, which was not available to Aquinas. All Scotus has to establish is that there is no need to think that an infinite regress of essentially ordered causes is metaphysically necessary. If it is not necessary, then its opposite is possible. And if it is possible that there is a first cause (because the absence of such a cause is not metaphysically necessary) then he has all he needs for this argument to go through. The burden of proof then lies with those who would maintain that an infinite regress of essentially ordered causes is not merely possible but necessary. I know of no such proof.

This leaves the first premise. Why should we think that God's possibility in the real order is enough to establish God's existence in the real order? The argument goes as follows:

1. Whatever is possible in the real order is either actual or causable in the real order.
2. God is not causable. Therefore
3. God is actual in the real order.

Why is God not causable? Because an uncaused first cause cannot itself be caused on pain of contradiction. Anything caused ipso facto fails to be God. This was Avicenna's original point. So we are left with the conclusion that if God is so much as possible in the real order, there being nothing in the alleged nature of God that is repugnant to being, and such an entity being required to explain what we know to actually be the case, then God must be actual: for only if God is actual can God be so much as possible. So those who would maintain that God does not exist must show that God is not even a metaphysical possibility. This is to turn the tables on Oppy entirely.

Now, whatever one thinks of these arguments, they are not foolish, simple-minded or theologically dogmatic; and they do not fall to the standard criticisms of cosmological and ontological arguments. Their premises are not obviously false. The arguments themselves are formally valid. They do not appear to violate any principles of naturalism. So there appears to be no reason to deny that these arguments meet the standards of cogency philosophers routinely expect serious arguments to meet. So these arguments need not be a stumbling block to the serious philosopher. Indeed these arguments succeed in shifting the burden of proof onto the non-theist. Those who would reject these arguments must show

a. that there can be vague entities in the real order, not just vague concepts. Keeping to scholastic standards, this entails showing that there *are* entities in the real order for which the principles of bivalence and non-contradiction to do not apply, or

b that an infinite regress of essentially ordered causes is metaphysically necessary, not just a theoretical possibility, or what amounts to the same thing,

c that an ontologically basic entity or level is metaphysically impossible.

It would be very interesting indeed to see cogent arguments for any of these claims.

CHAPTER SIX

Scholasticism and Western 'disenchantment'

Weber contends that modern Western civilization is 'disenchanted' because our society's method of arriving at beliefs about the world, that is, the sciences, is unable to address questions of value. The result is that we are prone to anti-realist views regarding value, forms of relativism, and even nihilism. The Western world is thus in the strange position of being ever more able to manipulate nature to our own ends, thus raising our standard of living beyond anything imaginable even 100 years ago, while having to maintain that our ends are ultimately quite pointless, and our causes never just. This final chapter illustrates how scholastic metaphysical principles eliminate the root cause of our disenchantment. If scholasticism can treat Weberian disenchantment convincingly, then the case for medieval philosophy rests.

Introduction

My case for scholasticism is nearly at an end; but one more very important topic remains. As mentioned in the opening chapter of this book, one of the key tensions of our current social order is that our preferred method of arriving at authoritative knowledge claims about the natural and social orders, namely, the sciences, is unable to speak to values, including the values that underpin the institutions of our political and economic orders. The result is that we lack any socially sanctioned means of justifying or critiquing objectively our commitment to the characteristic elements of our political and economic orders. That is, we can never claim to know that our social order is 'just', 'right' or 'better' than alternative social orders, or that it is 'unjust', 'wrong' or 'worse' than alternative social orders. Thus we are faced with the curious and uncomfortable fact that certain institutions of our own social order force the judgement that significant components of that same social order necessarily lack objective legitimacy. This is bad enough. But if there should prove to be tensions between our political and economic orders, as indeed there are, we are at a loss when it comes to knowing what adjustments to make because no adjustment is objectively justified by the sciences any more than any other. As Weber says, it is this lack of legitimacy that deprives our actions in the private and public spheres of any satisfying meaning. Living in a meaningless order, however successful that order might be in other respects, is to be disenchanted.

In good times legitimacy issues can perhaps be overlooked. But in periods of crisis, such as those we have been experiencing in the West since 2008,[1] concerns about legitimacy will surface. And the West is currently undergoing a crisis of confidence regarding the main elements of the political and economic orders. This is playing out most clearly in the political sphere where, in country after country, the political establishment is losing out to anti-establishment movements of both the left and the right.[2] These popular movements have asserted themselves through the ballot box, as is entirely in accordance with the political institutions of our social order. But the appeal of these movements in many cases rests on their promise to do away with policies that are integral to the institutions of our economic order. Protectionist tendencies, the most prominent element of the anti-establishment movements, are at odds with the West's official commitment to an economic system which encourages the free movement of goods, services, capital and people.[3] What is more, by curtailing these freedoms, these anti-establishment movements are also at odds with the official political sentiment in favour of governments letting their citizens live their lives according to their own lights as much as possible.

In short, whether one welcomes or deplores these developments, the fact remains that our political and economic orders are no longer in harmony. And so we have two significant aporia at the level of the social order. The first, and most pressing, is that our cognitive order undermines the legitimacy of our political and economic orders, resulting in disenchantment. The second, a corollary of the first, is that we are at a loss as to how to justify any adjustments we might make to restore harmony between the political and economic orders, for the sciences sanction no adjustment any more than any other. But just what adjustments are going to be made in these orders constitutes the drama of our times. And drama there will be because, alas, it is no longer possible to maintain in all seriousness that there is a harmony of economic and political interests between all nations and between the individuals of these nations, as was perhaps the case in the nineteenth century. This means that any mooted adjustment will produce winners and losers, hence the moral import of these questions: Which adjustments should be made to our social order? How does one decide whose losses are worth incurring and whose are not, and at what price? And how are these adjustments to be justified and rendered legitimate?[4]

In the opening chapter of this book I argued that a philosophy that matters will be a philosophy that is able to speak meaningfully to aporia that emerge at the level of the social order. Now I am *not* suggesting that a philosophy that matters will solve these aporia for us. For reasons that will become clear below, resolving these dilemmas will involve significant *empirical* work in addition to the more conceptually oriented work of philosophers. What I am suggesting is that *a philosophy that matters should provide a conceptual framework in which solutions can become visible, thereby focussing our attention in fruitful directions*. Now part of the challenge facing contemporary philosophy as a discipline is precisely that it has talked itself into a position where it is unable to offer any assistance on these matters. Our dilemmas are rooted in the fact that we have trained ourselves and others to believe that the natural and social sciences have nothing to say about questions of value. This makes it impossible to have a rational debate about these most pressing questions because one cannot carefully gather all the relevant information, and then marshal arguments in favour of a policy proposal on the basis of that information,[5] for such an argument would constitute a piece of objective moral knowledge, precisely what we cannot have according to the standard account of the sciences. But if moral knowledge is impossible, how do we legitimize our policy proposals?

Let us first acknowledge that the most effective way of legitimizing *any* social order is to remove the temptation to question it in the first place. This temptation arises whenever there is a widespread sense that a social order is failing to deliver. The proximate cause of anxiety at the moment is the feeling that globalization has not been an unmitigated good, particularly for certain sectors of the economy in developed countries. To address these anxieties countries in the West must find ways to boost productivity, wages and workplace participation. If this can be done without incurring gross injustices, legitimacy issues will become academic for all practical purposes. Nothing succeeds like success.

But we do not live by bread and circuses alone. Eventually the consequences of sundering the cognitive from the political and economic orders will resurface. When they do, what will philosophy have to offer? The answer, in our current dispensation at least, is, 'Not much'. The unseemly but entirely predictable result is that we are reduced to the level of 'post-truth politics'. If the 'official' line is that moral knowledge is impossible, why worry about facts and truths? And why worry about what 'experts' might have to say about these facts? If facts cannot be used to justify policies, facts can (and perhaps should) be ignored. What 'justifies' a policy proposal in our current dispensation is something else entirely, namely, its incorporating a 'value' we happen to share. The consequence is that our political and social interactions are increasingly confined to signalling our values to one another in order to attract like-valued people who 'identify' with us, rather than thinking rigorously about policy proposals. And politicians have followed suit. They engage in value signalling themselves rather than running on genuine policy proposals.[6] Ultimately cynicism and disenchantment win out, for what we euphemistically call our 'values' are really just our interests. Political and economic policy is thus decided by who is able to get their interest/value/identity group to the ballot box in the greatest numbers in the right districts. This is arguably still the best way to arrive at political decisions. Counting heads is still better than breaking them, even if they are inevitably cynical heads.[7] But electoral victory in this dispensation is hollow, for we are forever reminded of the fact that, objectively, all interest/values/identities are on a moral par. No victory at the ballot box proves that a cause is just. This cannot fail to undermine the legitimacy of the democratic process itself.[8]

In this final chapter I want to lay out a scholastic framework for thinking about ethical matters that hold out the promise of treating Weberian disenchantment. This means finding a way to forge a connection between facts and values. But I begin by tracing the roots of disenchantment so that we can understand the origins of the illness we are seeking to treat. This done I can then lay out a scholastic ethics. We can then see how a scholastic would handle the lines of thought that got us into trouble in the first place. If this can be done in a compelling fashion, then the case for scholasticism can rest.

How did we get into this fine mess?

Before considering what the scholastics have to offer regarding disenchantment it is worth reviewing the most influential lines of thought in support of the claim that moral knowledge is impossible, for let there be no mistake: it is because moral knowledge is deemed impossible that the most serious legitimacy issues arise. The first point to note about these arguments is their provenance: these arguments come from virtually all of the diverse sectors of our fractured discipline. Moreover, they combine metaphysical, epistemological and socio-political considerations to build a comprehensive defence of moral anti-realism and scepticism. Indeed it is difficult to avoid the conclusion that the discipline of philosophy itself has been a significant sponsor of disenchantment. If ever there was a case of philosophy mattering beyond the halls of academe, it is here.

So why do we think that facts are one thing, values another, and that never the twain shall meet? It is worth listing the most historically effective arguments for this claim:

1 Moore's Open Question Argument taught us that moral facts cannot be natural facts. So, if there are moral facts they must be non-natural facts. But non-natural facts are metaphysically dubious. And even if non-natural facts were metaphysically respectable, it is not clear that human beings could ever have reliable cognitive access to them. So there are no moral facts, and so no moral knowledge.[9]

2 If there were moral facts, they would be very strange things indeed. For if there were objectively good or bad states

of affairs, say, these states of affairs would have 'to-be-doneness' and 'not-to-be-doneness' somehow built into them. But mature scientific theories make no reference to such facts. And such facts would violate the standard view that beliefs about states of affairs are motivationally inert. So there are no moral facts, and so no moral knowledge.[10]

3. If there were moral facts, then there would be convergence of moral opinion amongst morally competent judges. There is no such convergence. The best explanation for this lack of convergence is that there are no moral facts. Ergo, there are no moral facts and no moral knowledge.

These are the core arguments for anti-realism, that is, the claim that the real order does not contain states of affairs in virtue of which moral judgements are true or false. An additional argument for moral scepticism – the view that there might very well be mind-independent moral facts, but we can never know what they are – depends on the fact–value gap:

4. For a moral judgement to count as knowledge it must be justified. It will be justified either by another moral claim which itself will require justification, or by a factual claim. But no moral claim follows from a factual claim or set of such claims. But the regress of justifications by further moral claims is infinite, leaving the initial claim unjustified. So moral knowledge is impossible.

Then there are socio-political considerations which militate against the *desirability* of acknowledging the very possibility of moral knowledge:

5. It is undesirable to acknowledge the possibility of moral facts, and so the possibility of moral knowledge, because of the following:

   i. *This would transform* moral and political problems into technical problems to be solved by experts. This leads to moral amnesia. And,
   ii. Knowledge is power, and moral knowledge in particular sanctions a power that could (will? always?) prove oppressive.

These have been amongst the most influential contributions to meta-ethics from philosophy since the publication of Moore's *Principia Ethica*. Far from being helpful in dealing with disenchantment, they positively re-enforce it. But if disenchantment is a problem, and there is little in the way of remedy coming from contemporary philosophy, then, if scholasticism proves useful in this respect, we will have shown yet again that scholasticism matters beyond the halls of academe.

A scholastic ethical theory

In this section I will set out in a fairly condensed fashion *a* scholastic ethical theory, for the scholastics did not all sing from the same meta-ethical hymn sheet. However, all were realists of some description or another. That is, all agreed that moral judgements had mind-independent truth-makers; at issue was what these truth-makers were and how we might know them. Now if a plausible and compelling form of moral realism could be gleaned from the scholastics, then their relevance to contemporary concerns would be transparent. I believe that a form of realism fitting the bill is to be had from the scholastics, in particular in Aquinas's theory of practical reason. In the interest of keeping the scholastics in touch with contemporary sensibilities, I will focus on a naturalist account of his natural law theory that keeps theological considerations out of the picture. This is entirely appropriate since the natural law theorist in the Thomist tradition is tasked with providing a foundation for ethics acceptable to all rational people independently of faith considerations.[11]

The first point to emphasize here is that scholastic moral realism has its roots, not in ethics, but in metaphysics. In keeping with most ancient moral traditions, the idea is to begin with a background metaphysical understanding of the universe and our place in it, and then work towards an account of how human beings should live, both privately and collectively. And the most important point for our purposes is that there is no room in the scholastic metaphysical framework for the fact–value distinction that lies at the heart of much modern moral thinking. And the reason for this is that the facts about the natural order that prove central to scholastic metaphysical and epistemological frameworks are identical to the facts that ground their ethical judgements. To use the language of a previous chapter, there is only a mental distinction, not a real distinction, between facts and values.

As we saw in Chapter 1, the characteristic element of scholastic metaphysics is the notion of form. To do justice to the common sense belief that the world contains changing, middle-sized objects it was necessary to distinguish between an object's matter and form. Form, the arrangement or pattern according to which the matter of an object is organized, is what makes that object the kind of thing it is, and provides its existence and identity conditions. An object's form is also crucial from an epistemological point of view because form has an explanatory function. An object's properties and causal powers, its capacities and developmental trajectory, are all due to its form. What an object can become, what sorts of changes it can go through, what sorts of changes it can bring about in other things, all depend on what it is, that is, on its form. And it is this same form which has a central role in ethics because the highest good of living creatures such as ourselves – our ultimate happiness, our flourishing, our well-being – lies in our most perfect operation,[12] operations which are grounded in and determined by our form. Achieving this most perfect operation in living things requires the unfolding and development of our form from the stages of fertilized embryo to fully functioning adult. This development can go well, or it can be hindered and stymied.

Now, in this framework, ethics is the discipline devoted to specifying what these operations are, and what sorts of actions and character traits, as well as social and political institutions, constitute, help or hinder human flourishing and well-being. And these were taken to be matters of fact, not matters of value. There was, of course, still plenty of room for debate in the ancient world. To the central questions – What is the best life for human beings? What constitutes human flourishing? – competing answers were given. Much debate centred on the credentials of various candidate lives, such as (a) the life devoted to money making in the interests of securing pleasure (a popular view amongst the general public); (b) the life devoted to public service in the interest of securing honour (popular amongst aristocrats); (c) the life devoted to contemplation (favoured by Aristotle) and (d) the life of tranquillity and peace of mind (favoured by the Epicureans and Sceptics). But we need not get into these debates here. Much time can be saved if we focus on the *preconditions* of *any* of these candidate lives. And the key precondition is *health*, physical, emotional and psycho-social. Health is both a constituent feature of flourishing, and a precondition of any further operations that make up a good life.

Now the conditions necessary to promote and preserve health in human beings are uncontroversial. These necessities include whatever preserves human life, like adequate nutrition, potable water, serviceable clothing, shelter and fuel (the so-called 'Malthusian necessities'), and whatever preserves human society and the benefits derived from the social order, like security (domestic and social), access to healthcare and access to education, to name only a few examples.[13] Once these basic necessities are secured on a reliable basis we can then enter into a second-level debate about which of the various lives on offer is the best. But the point here is that all of these necessities stem from our nature, from our form. If our form were otherwise, then our needs would be different.

Now my suggestion is that by relying on the notion of form, which lies at the heart of scholastic metaphysics, epistemology *and* ethics, we can begin to take seriously a theory of practical rationality, the basic principles of which are as follows:[14]

- **i** Our desiderata as ethical theorists are objective principles of practical rationality that allow us to distinguish between *reasonable* (right) and *unreasonable* (wrong) actions.[15]
- **ii** A reason for acting is some possible *good* to be pursued or a possible *bad* to be avoided.[16]
- **iii** Something is a good if it promotes human health, physical, emotional, psychological and social. Something is a bad if it hinders human health.[17]
- **iv** An action is reasonable/right if it is a *non-defective response to a good.*
- **v** A response is non-defective if (a) it is a token of a *kind* of action which tends to maintain and promote the widespread distribution of goods amongst those affected by the action;[18] (b) a *token* of that kind is appropriate in the specific *circumstances* of the action[19] and (c) the primary *intention* motivating the agent is to bring about the good associated with actions of that kind.[20]

vi Conditions (a), (b) and (c) are individually necessary and jointly sufficient for an action to be right. Failure in any one respect entails a defective response to a good.[21]

vii There are degrees of defectiveness. Sometimes what one does is objectively defective, but the act might remain acceptable, if not wholly so, because it is the least defective response available in the circumstances.

viii There is a hierarchy of goods.[22]

ix Because what constitutes human health is determined by a universal human nature, the principles of practical rationality are universally binding.[23]

x These principles are knowable largely through empirical means. That is, rightness and wrongness are *not* determined by a priori reflection, *nor* by appeals to gut level intuitions, *nor* by ideological commitments. Putative principles are tested against experience to determine whether they are 'conducive to well-living'.[24]

Now space considerations make it impossible to defend this theory in any detail here. But the important point for our present purposes is that this theory provides a framework for responsible deliberation and discussion of social, political and economic policies because it allows facts to speak to values. The objective facts relating to human health broadly construed are the facts that measure the moral value of our actions, policies and institutions. The objective facts I have in mind include increased life expectancy at birth; a decrease in infant/mother mortality rates; a decrease in morbidity rates; an increase in literacy and numeracy rates; an increase in per capital income (GDP); an increase in gender empowerment. Moreover, this theory points us in the right direction. Ascertaining precisely these facts across societies and time periods is part of the empirical and historical work that needs to be done to assess the merits of social dispensations. Also necessary is to determine empirically whether a policy in one context necessarily has the same results when implemented in another. What works in one context might not work in another, and only empirical study can settle such matters. But the point here is that this framework of practical reasoning directs us to particular objective features of social orders, and gives a means of assessing them objectively with a view to human well-being.

To be clear, this framework eschews the 'positivism' that has been at the heart of modern science and the modern economist's self-image in the Anglo-American sphere. It is no longer feasible or desirable to pretend to be morally neutral in the intimately related fields of economics and politics.[25] Nor will it do for the economist to rely on a version of preference utilitarianism in the hope that this will absolve us of having to think seriously about ethical matters, for ethics is not just about counting preferences.[26] Now this theory of practical reason with roots in the natural law tradition allows one to reconnect political and economic policy with serious ethical reflection.[27] It also takes us back to the origins of the scientific study of economics and the late scholastics of the School of Salamanca;[28] it brings back into focus the role of natural law in Adam Smith's thought,[29] and, just as importantly, it suggests that the ordoliberalism of Walter Eucken, particularly his thoughts on the value of an economic constitution, is a promising place to start one's efforts to re-think economic matters on a sound ethical footing.[30]

But equally clearly, this framework does *not* eschew the sciences per se. This is the first ingredient in the scholastic solution to our current difficulties – disenchantment is an illusion. There is no philosophically respectable argument that justifies claiming that the empirical reports of the sciences can have no relation to our value judgements or to our practical reasoning. This was just a mistake, and a bad one at that. What is important is that we rely on respectable science; that we become scientifically literate ourselves, particularly with respect to scientific method, statistics and experimental design; and that we do not rely on the overly sensationalist reporting on science that dominates the media. This is not to defect from the sciences. On the contrary, it is to buttress the sciences so that they can do more than we previously suspected. This is possible if we recognize that the sciences need to be supported by the principles of scholastic metaphysics. This means that we can hope that empirical studies about which economic and political policies lead to improvements in human well-being, and under what conditions, can serve as the basis of responsible, objectively legitimate, social institutions, practices and policy decisions. Odd as it sounds, employing a 'medieval' philosophical framework is the best way we have of keeping faith with modernity.

If this is a way to address the core aporia of modernity – the cleaving of the cognitive from the economic and political orders – is there anything the scholastics have to offer on the others? Bearing in mind the need to address these tensions in context, and the need to consider policies from an empirical point of view, the following general pointers can be suggested as places to start thinking seriously about the challenges of modernity.

Generally what we have seen in this book is that when scholastics face an aporia they try to find a way to save each of the individually plausible lines of thought that lead to the appearance of a puzzle. My suggestion here is that we try to follow the scholastics play book in our current case. Rather than defect from any of the ingredients of our current social order, we should 'double down' on all of them, strengthening them rather than abandoning them.

Recall that the first tension between the political and economic orders stems from the fact that political power is held at the national level (bestowed in national elections), while economic power is now a global phenomenon (in line with our commitment to market economics). The problem is that the electorate expects our politicians to deal with problems that lie outwith their control. Politicians are then tempted to defect from our economic images and cling to nationalism and protectionism (Brexit and Trump are prime examples) or even to look at the 'China model'. Secondly, the electorate expects national governments to provide a range of services, but is seldom willing to shoulder the financial costs these services incur. Politicians are then tempted to borrow to pay for services, deferring the payment to subsequent generations, running the risk of financial ruin. National indebtedness has become acute in many 'Western style' democracies. Tackling it is very difficult for politicians who will face the electorate at the polls in short order. The same can be said for economic policies regarding the environment. We all want 'green policies' but few are willing to pay for them even if questions of practicality are set aside.

No doubt there is much pressure at the moment to defect from our economic images, and retreat behind protectionist policies in the hope that states can thereby regain a degree of national sovereignty. Alternatively, one might think we need to reconsider our commitment to democratic principles. History suggests we should do neither. Trade ultimately improves the lives of everyone, as economic history has shown. And the last time we considered abandoning democratic principles (in the wake of the First World War, the Russian Revolution and the collapse of the Weimar

Republic) the West entered what was unquestionably the most turbulent, not to say utterly disastrous, times in our political history.

My suggestion is to double down on our political images of democracy and constitutionalism, *and* the market mechanism for non-public goods. Taking the political image first, we ought not to defect from democracy, or even move to limit the franchise, but widen it still further. The problem is not too much democracy, but too little. Key to the difficulty we find ourselves in is that our elections are dominated by only a section of those whose interests are involved. But those who hold political power should rule on behalf of *all* those affected by their decisions. But currently even our most representative democracies are dominated by the tyranny of the *present* electorate, that is, those eligible to vote *now*. This inevitably leads to the enforced short-sightedness of our politicians who can never see beyond the next election. This means that under our current arrangements the interests of future generations count for nothing, because the future has no lobby, and the current electorate always prefers jam today to jam tomorrow. Thus our current dispensation does not live up to our political images. In order to remedy this we need to find a way of ensuring that our politicians arrive at decisions that privilege present needs over future needs (because present need is more urgent than a future need that has yet to materialize) but not present wants over future needs.

How might the votes of future generations be counted in today's elections if they aren't here to vote? One suggestion is to use a technique we are already familiar with. We know that no future generation will vote for policies that threaten to impoverish it, or for policies that threaten the sustainability of the social order and the sustainability of the natural environment on which life on this planet depends. So one suggestion would be to enshrine these points in an *economic constitution* which makes policies that threaten future needs unconstitutional and illegal. This would protect politicians from the present electorate which would otherwise have them over-spend or engage in irresponsible behaviour. We accept the principle that not everything that is popular is constitutional or legal, and we do not see this as limiting in an unacceptable way the powers of our political rulers. The same should be enforced in the political sphere with reference to fiscal and monetary policy. This would undermine the force of the claim that democracies with an expanded franchise must always court economic disaster: not necessarily so. A democracy that expands the electorate still further can heed the interests of future generations, and behave accordingly.

What about the tension between political power being held at the national level while economic power is global? Again, we should double down on our economic and political images. Protectionism has only ever served narrow, short-term, special interests. We need to stand firm on this fact of economic history. But those in power are tempted to satisfy those interests because they are loudly proclaimed in the run up to elections. And, of course, it behoves politicians to do what they can for those affected by their decisions. But their decisions need to take into account everyone who is affected by them. And while special interests groups have their lobbies, the needs of the general consumer, who suffers from higher prices under protectionism, and the nation, which suffers from a loss of competitiveness, are often forgotten in the clamour of elections. We need our politicians to arrive at decisions that take everyone's interests into account, not just those of a special interest. And this means that we need politicians to be able to arrive at decisions that (i) privilege the needs of the nation as a whole, not the wants or even the needs of special interests (for the whole is greater than the part), but at the same time, (ii) we need our politicians to be able to arrive at decisions that privilege national needs over the needs of non-nationals (needs closer to home have a greater call on our resources than those at some remove). But, analogous to the previous case, the wants of nationals should not trump the needs of non-nationals. Not only is it imprudent to ignore difficulties abroad, it is a moral disgrace not to do what we can for others when doing so does not compromise our welfare. These points too can be enshrined in the economic constitution. But ultimately we must go with what proves to be the most effective policies in terms of securing human welfare, and this is decided empirically.

A scholastic response to objections

Of course one might object that this theory of practical reason completely violates the fact–value distinction, and commits the naturalist fallacy in the most egregious manner. And, of course, it does. But this is a problem *only* if the fact–value distinction is sound, and the naturalist fallacy is really a fallacy. But they are not.

We have already had occasion to considered Moore's Open Question Argument in Chapter 4. It was noted that Moore mistakes a mental distinction for a real distinction. Contra Moore and his followers, the Open Question Argument provides no reason to believe that moral facts are really distinct from natural facts. This undercuts the need to place moral facts in a non-natural realm. And since they do not reside in some realm inaccessible to human cognition, there are no special worries about our cognitive access to these facts. We access them like any other natural facts, empirically. So those familiar with scholastic work on the nature of distinctions will be unmoved by the Open Question Argument.[31]

What about the 'argument from queerness'? The scholastic should reply that this argument is based on an unwarranted account of what a moral fact needs to be. Why believe that objectively good or bad states of affairs have 'to-be-doneness' and 'not-to-be-doneness' built into them any more than air has 'to-be-breathedness' built into it? Why would lacking such admittedly queer features preclude certain states of affairs being objectively good or bad for human health and well-being? The reply appears to be that appeal to such queer facts is the only way to explain the phenomenon of the moral imperative, that is, the sense that some actions are absolutely obligatory and some absolutely forbidden regardless of our desires. But this consideration lacks force if other plausible explanations of this sense are available. Is it not open to one to say that our motivations and attitudes to things and states of affairs follow our perceptions of what is good and bad for human health and well-being? When we care deeply about our good (as we usually do) and we perceive that an action is necessary to attain that good or to avoid some bad, then, even if that action has undesirable features, we tend to feel as though 'we can do no other', particularly if the good or bad in question is highly significant. In this scenario the 'authority' of a moral judgement is rooted in our *appreciation* of the significance of the good in question.[32] But the fact that moral authority lies in our appreciation of the significance of something does not stop that thing from being objectively good or bad for human health and well-being. After all, it is not our attitude to states of affairs that makes those states of affairs good or bad. The direction of fit is precisely the reverse. What makes a pro-attitude to a state of affairs appropriate is that that state of affairs is objectively good for human health and well-being. Indeed, if someone is *not* motivated by such states of affairs, this reflects on their character or their state of mind, not the states of affairs themselves. To ask for more than this as an explanation of the moral imperative smacks of holding out for a special 'moral ought'. But as Anscombe pointed out in the middle of the last century, this is a religious hangover we need to learn to do without.[33]

What about the argument from the relativity of moral judgements? If there are objective, natural moral facts, why is there no consensus amongst competent judges on moral matters? There are numerous ways to counter this argument. The first is to point out that our attention is usually drawn to cases of disagreement, while cases of agreement tend to be taken for granted. Moral disagreements do exist, but they are in fact a tiny fraction of the moral judgements we make on which we all agree. The extent of moral disagreement is thus often grossly exaggerated and the extent of the consensus underplayed. Secondly, one can insist that a widespread moral consensus is a necessary condition of our being able to even notice the disagreements we do have.[34] Thirdly, one can point to the fact that moral judgements can be fiendishly difficult, if only because we usually have to act on imperfect or incomplete information. In such cases it is not particularly surprising that competent and sincere judges can disagree on morally significant matters. Fourthly, it is important to recognize that circumstances are crucial. What is objectively right in one context can be objectively wrong in another without its compromising moral realism. But if one is not sensitive to the moral salience of context this fact can strike the unsophisticated as tantamount to relativism in the anti-realist sense. But this is just an elementary mistake. And finally, one should point out that moral judges are not always sincere, and the integrity of our moral debates is often compromised by a conflict of interests on the part of the participants. As Thracymachus, Nietzsche, Marx and Freud have taught us, whenever interests are in play, as they so often are in cases of moral disagreements, our cognitive faculties are not always employed honourably,[35] and even when they are, what we report as the upshot of our moral reflections is often entirely self-serving.[36] The upshot of these considerations is that we do *not* need to deny the existence of natural, mind-independent moral facts to account for moral disagreements. There are other perfectly good explanations.

What should we say about the argument for scepticism? Non-scholastic defenders of moral knowledge tend to accept the fact–value distinction on which this argument rests. They then insist either that some moral judgements are self-evident (as the intuitionists did in the early days of the twentieth century) or that justification can be achieved using coherentist strategies (Rawl's so-called 'wide reflective equilibrium strategy' has been a popular example). But intuitionism has proved difficult to defend, and always has a whiff of the mysterious about it. And coherentist strategies never entirely free themselves of the charge of circularity. The best approach is simply to reject the assumption underlying the standard use of the fact–value distinction on which the argument is based. The scholastic will grant that there is no *conceptual* connection between facts and values, so it is indeed impossible to arrive *deductively* at conclusions containing a value term from premises containing no such terms. And this is because, as Moore noted, there is *mental* distinction between natural terms and value terms. But if one accepts that there need be no *real* distinction between facts and values simply because there is a mental distinction between natural and value terms, then this point of logic is of no consequence.

What should the scholastic say to the socio-political point about the very desirability of moral knowledge? The scholastic ought to grant that moral knowledge can be difficult to attain, and that it is also possible that this knowledge can be abused. But it seems better to acknowledge these facts of life, and take steps to deal with them, than to claim that all social dispensations are on a moral par, for such a claim has particularly pernicious consequences. By denying that moral knowledge is possible, one undermines *both* the possibility of objectively critiquing the status quo, *and* the possibility of objectively defending alternative dispensations. Obviously this suits those happy with the status quo, for anyone trying to bring about change can be accused of causing social disruption in pursuit of their own interests. Thus, as surprising as it may sound, the social progressive must insist on the possibility of moral knowledge if they are to have any legitimacy. That this point runs counter to the obligatory relativism and postmodernism of many progressive activists and academics merely underlines how intellectually shallow and fashion conscious 'intellectuals' can be.

By contrast, the scholastic solution to the problem of disenchantment is to invite us back to serious moral reflection.

It is possible to show objectively that a social order is good or bad by examining its record of achievement for its people on those issues related to health, physical, emotional and psycho-social. This approach to ethics demands attention to empirical matters; it demands that morally responsible people inform themselves of the history of their own social order; of the merits and deficiencies of each element of their own social order; of the merits and deficiencies of alternative social orders, both possible and actual. All of this is demanding. It might even require a level of expertise that is currently so unfashionable. But it is worthwhile. And it can be uplifting: just the tonic for disenchantment.

But to accept the scholastic solution requires that philosophers face up to something we all know but rarely mention, namely, that there is no 'Whig' history of philosophy. The history of our beloved discipline is *not* one of slow but steady progress towards an ever greater approximation to the truth of things. Our history is much more akin to Kuhn's account of scientific progress, of one paradigm replacing another, usually for less than fully evidential or truth-related reasons. New philosophical mindsets initially gain traction within the discipline, and then take hold of generations of thinkers, not necessarily because they are improvements on what went before, but because they are 'timely', that is, because they somehow chime with and speak to contemporaneous issues of extra-philosophical concern in a compelling fashion. This means that perfectly respectable philosophical paradigms can go out of fashion for no good philosophical reason. This, I contend, is what happened to scholasticism in the transition from late medieval times to early modernity. But fashions have been known to return. What I hope to have shown in this work is that scholasticism is once again both philosophically respectable and timely.

NOTES

Introduction

1 These dates are no longer as stable as they once were. See Appendix I for a discussion of the boundaries of the Middle Ages.

2 I would recommend Wulf's *History of Medieval Philosophy* (Wulf, 1909) to anyone interested in getting a lengthy but comprehensive overview of medieval philosophy in its entirety.

3 Hawking and Mlodinow (2010, p. 5).

4 For those interested in how religion, philosophy and the sciences address similar issues see Stevenson (2004). In this very readable book he compares and contrasts Confucianism, Hinduism, Judaism, Christianity, Plato, Aristotle, Kant, Sartre, Marx, Freud and Darwin.

5 A similar challenge was felt by theologians when the complete Aristotelian corpus was recovered in the thirteenth century. If philosophy studies all of reality, as Aristotle claims, what is left to the theologian? This problem is raised in the first article of the very first question of Aquinas's *Summa Theologiae*: 'Everything that is, is considered in the philosophical disciplines – even God himself; so that there is a part of philosophy called theology, or the divine science, as is clear from Aristotle. Therefore besides the philosophical disciplines, there is no need of any further doctrine.'

6 Many specialists of medieval thought are now tempted to this last position. In the final chapter of his *Medieval Philosophy: A Very Short Introduction*, Marenbon (2016) suggests that the main point of studying medieval thought is to gain purely historical knowledge. He makes the point that familiarity with the history of philosophy in general is vital if one is to understand the world (insofar as ideas play a role in history). And since medieval philosophy is a part of this history, it too needs to be studied. In this book I want to go further than making this (obviously) correct but rather modest claim.

7 See DeLanda (2015, p. ix).

8 The tensions between general relativity theory and quantum mechanics are perhaps the most eye-catching example. But this is not the only case. Evolutionary biology and Chomsky's linguistics is another. The neurosciences do not sit well with any discipline that adverts to mental states like beliefs and desires to explain behaviour, putting it at odds with economics. And there are internal disputes in chemistry between standard accounts of the atom and the claims of quantum chemistry.

9 Of course it is not just professional philosophers who do this kind of thing, but the philosopher's standard training does provide the kinds of tools necessary for aporia resolution. Scientists with a theoretical orientation also do this kind of work. But when they do they are wearing the philosopher's hat and are no longer acting as scientists per se.

10 This is a compressed account of the nature of philosophical questions. For a fuller discussion see chapter 1 of Boulter (2007).

11 A non-scientific example will help. Say someone claims to have seen a ghost. You, as a good respecter of science, take the observation seriously; after all, observation is the basis of all genuine knowledge. But you, as a good respecter of science, are not likely to believe that anyone has actually seen a ghost. Why not? Because you don't believe in the *possibility* of ghosts. (Note, it is not just that you don't believe in ghosts. The issue is that you do not believe that ghosts are possible, in the same sense that you do not believe that square circles are possible.) So you will claim that, whatever this person saw, it wasn't a ghost. It couldn't have been a ghost because ghosts are impossible entities, and one cannot see what cannot exist. The point here is that what one takes to be possible determines how one interprets what one actually observes. The general argument, but not the example, is due to Lowe (2001, p. 5). See also Lowe (2007, p. 5).

12 See in particular Kuhn (1974).

13 See Duhem (1977) for a perceptive and detailed account of scientific theory shorn of metaphysical baggage. A key point of Duhem's masterpiece is that the price of eschewing metaphysical commitments in physics itself is the adoption of an anti-realist attitude vis-à-vis the theories of physics.

14 See chapter 1 of Gellner (1988). This division of the social order goes back to at least Plato's *Republic*, and also famously features in Adalberon of Loan's *Carmen ad Rotbertum regem*, where he separates society into the three estates: *oratores*, *bellatores* and *laboratores*. It is also echoes Talcott Parson's categories of 'goal-attainment' (the coercive/political), 'adaptation' (the productive)

and 'integration' (cognitive/legitimative), although it does leave unmentioned Parson's category of 'latency' (motivating individuals to adopt a role in one of these sub-systems). See chapter 2 of Parson (1991), particularly the section entitled The Functional Prerequisites of Social Systems. This division is also something of a commonplace amongst historians. Consider these comments about the changes to the social order brought about in Northern Europe during the Enlightenment period: 'The Enlightenment project ... consists of two projects, a political one that would create a better society and a philosophical one that would replace religion with rational thought and an understanding of Nature. There was a third project, however, namely to make the economy produce more wealth and thus to increase what economists today call economic welfare' (Mokyr, 2009, p. 30). The contrasts in the cognitive/legitimative, political and economic orders used to highlight the key changes between pre- and post-Enlightenment Europe are consistent with the sociology.

15 See Weber (1926, pp. 347–8).

16 See Morgenthau (1993, p. 121).

17 For a recent discussion of this crisis see *Foreign Affairs*, Vol. 97, No. 3, May/June 2018. For book-length discussions see Deneen (2018) and Galston (2018).

18 Often rapidly and unexpectedly, as happened in the case of the Soviet Union.

19 Perhaps the best example of this tension is the so-called Mundell–Fleming trilemma. Governments working within a globalized economy have to choose between the following incompatible desiderata: (i) free capital mobility, (ii) monetary autonomy and (iii) exchange rate management. In an ideal world a government would be able to have all three simultaneously as this would allow governments a measure of control over the forces that shape the lives of their citizens. But the reality is that one must choose which of the three desiderata to drop.

20 Weber writes, 'The fate of our times is characterised by rationalisation and intellectualisation and, above all, by "the disenchantment of the world". Precisely the ultimate and most sublime values have retreated from public life into either the transcendental realms of mystic life or into the brotherliness of direct and personal human relations' (in Gerth and Mills, 1946, pp. 129–56).

21 The following account of Weber relies heavily on Lessnoff (1999), chapter 2.

22 Schumpeter gives a particularly clear expression of this point. He writes,

> I fully agree with those who maintain that judgments about ultimate values – about the Common Good, for instance – are beyond the scientist's range except as objects of historical study, that they are ideologies by nature and that the concept of scientific progress can be applied to them only so far as the means may be perfected that are to implement them. I share the conviction that there is no sense is saying that the world of ideas of bourgeois liberalism is 'superior' in any relevant sense to the world of ideas of the middle ages, or the world of ideas of socialism to that of bourgeois liberalism. Actually, I further believe that there is no reason other than personal preference for saying that more wisdom or knowledge goes into our policies than went into those of the Tudors or Stuarts or, for that matter, into Charlemagne's.

Found in Hausman (2008, p. 211).

23 In fact it won't sound odd to everyone. This is precisely the thesis recently supported in Bain (2017).

Chapter one

1 Aristotle's struggle with the Socratic claim that no one ever does what they know to be wrong is perhaps the best known example of this attitude at work. Aristotle respects Socrates, as he should. But he also respects the views of the ordinary Athenian on the street who knows only too well that people frequently do what they know to be wrong. His challenge is to save Socrates's blushes by finding some sense in which the Socratic claim might be deemed correct, knowing that in its boldest formulation it simply cannot be right.

2 In fact the history of the origins of Cartesianism is quite complicated. For one view which finds its roots deep in the Middle Ages see Boulter (2011, pp. 617–41). More on this in Chapter 4.

3 For a recent example see Jaeger (2017), in which it is argued that a core Aristotelian notion of 'potentiality' proves useful in coming to terms with Heisenberg's interpretation of quantum mechanics. See also Boulter (2012, pp. 83–104).

4 I have discussed this issue at some length elsewhere, so I will not re-enter into all the details of this rather thorny question. For those interested in the technicalities please see chapter 1 of Boulter (2007).

5 See Strawson (2006, p. 10).

6 Not all real things are like this. Husbands and wives exist, but they are not part of the natural order because spouses are not mind independent the way the chemical elements are. And this is because a human is a husband or a wife not by nature but only if other humans come to see someone *as* a husband or a wife. Similarly a piece of paper counts as money only if we agree to treat it as money, and a ball crossing a line is a goal only if it crosses the line in accordance with our rules of football. Spouses, money and goals all exist, but they don't exist in the same way as the objects of the natural order. They are part of a socially constructed order. Now knowledge of the social order might very well be possible, but Proposition (11) is not committed to this.

7 Of course, there is more to knowledge than truth. But truth is a necessary, if not a sufficient, condition of knowledge.

8 Hence the vogue for tapestries that covered the windows of grand houses and manors to prevent the breeze bringing in the pestilence. See Cantor (2002) for a good study of this dreadful episode.

9 Plato had some exotic ideas on how to overcome this problem involving reincarnation and out-of-body experiences. Needless to say these haven't travelled well.

10 Developmental biology is that branch of biology devoted to understanding how complex organisms are built from a single fertilized egg. For the view that developmental programmes are forms in the Aristotelian sense see Boulter (2012, pp. 83–104).

11 'Immanent' means that the forms exist *in* material objects, not as separate abstract objects as Plato would have it. The Aristotelian position is that all singulars come in repeatable types due to the fact that one of their metaphysical parts is an immanent form. I say 'metaphysical part' advisedly, for this is perhaps the key distinguishing feature of the scholastic framework. This position distinguishes it from the metaphysical systems of Plato and Democritus, as well as those of the early modern period which can be characterized as a group as those which insist that material objects have only integral parts and no metaphysical parts. Aristotle's rejection of the atomism of Democritus, and the scholastic rejection of corpuscularism in the early modern period, is made on precisely the point that one cannot give an adequate account of a material object by adverting solely to its integral parts.

12 For a very clear statement of this position see Suarez (1964, pp. 70–3).

13 In the realm of concepts the innumerable details of reality are sacrificed on the altar of simplicity and generality. This process is one scientists are quite familiar with. Duhem's account of the role of physical laws in scientific thought is very close to the scholastics' parallel account of concepts. Duhem writes,

> The human mind had been facing an enormous number of concrete facts; no man could have embraced and retained a knowledge of all these facts; none could have communicated this knowledge to his fellows. Abstraction entered the scene. It brought about the removal of everything private or individual from these facts, extracting them from their total only what was general in them or common to them, and in place of this cumbersome mass of facts it has substituted a single proposition, occupying little of one's memory and easy to convey through instruction: it had formulated a physical law. (1977, p. 22)

14 Even John Scotus accepts this account as far as it goes. However, he notoriously goes further than an Aquinas or an Ockham by insisting that there is an extra-mental common nature which is not really but only formally distinct from singulars. But even he does not suggest that extra-mental reality contains universals in the strict sense.

15 This is what I take Lewis to be doing in his discussion of the problem of temporary intrinsic properties (1987, pp. 202–5). To allow for 'change' in intrinsic properties he has to say that 'different intrinsic properties ... belong to different things. ... There is no problem at all about how different things can differ in their intrinsic properties' (p. 204). This is undoubtedly true, but the point about change is that *one and the same thing* is to have different intrinsic properties at different times, not two distinct things, hence the assertion that perdurance theories in effect deny the reality of change.

16 See Lewis (2002, chapter 3) for a critical discussion of perdurance and temporal parts theories.

17 See Boulter (2007) for an extended defence of this Moorean approach to conflicts arising between common sense and philosophy.

18 The literature on Aristotle's metaphysics is very extensive and extraordinarily sophisticated, and there is, unsurprisingly, room for rational debate regarding the details of his position. What I

provide here, however, is relatively uncontroversial amongst Aristotle scholars. I follow the account given in Charles (2000), note 2.

19 It is not for nothing that Lawson-Tancred deemed Aristotle's 'the received metaphysics of the Western world' (in Aristotle (2004, p. xxiii)).

Chapter two

1 Good places to start are Duhem (1954, 1955). See also Thorndike (1923), Koyre (1956, pp. 1–22), Butterfield (1957), Hooykaas (1972), Dales (1973) and Blumenberg (1987). For a summary of more recent work see chapter 5 of Woods (2015). For comparative studies of the sciences in non-Western contexts see Needham (1954).

2 See le Goff (2007).

3 Interestingly enough, even at the level of particular theories continuity is to be found on occasion. The medieval notion of 'impetus' is perhaps the most widely discussed as being a precursor of the idea of inertia. Another particularly striking but lesser known example is in the field of economics. In his celebrated *History of Economic Analysis* Schumpeter (1954, chapter 3) points out that much of late scholastic economic thought is taken up unchanged by early modern economists.

4 On the order to be found in nature we find the following: *Wisdom* 11.21, 'thou hast *ordered* all things by measure and number and weight' and *Wisdom* 7.17–21, 'He himself gave me true understanding of things as they are: a knowledge of the structure of the world and the operation of the elements; the beginning and end of epochs and their middle course; the alternating solstices and changing seasons; the cycles of the years and the constellations; the nature of living creatures and the behaviour of wild beasts; the violent force of winds and the thoughts of men; the varieties of plants and the virtues of roots'. Here we are provided with an entire curriculum which is very much geared to the repeatable patterns or cycles in the natural order.

5 See Goldstein (1995, p. 77).

6 Indeed, apart from the celebrated case of Galileo, it is difficult to find instances in which the Church stymied early modern science.

7 This was one of the arguments used to motivate the 'insufficiency of the sciences' thesis of Chapter 1.

8 See Grice (1989, p. 26).

9 The co-operative principle is supplemented with the following maxims: (i) Make your contribution as informative as is required for the current purposes of the exchange. (ii) Do not make your contribution more informative than is required. (iii) Do not say what you believe to be false. (iv) Do not say that for which you lack adequate evidence. (v) Be relevant. (vi) Avoid obscurity of expression. (vii) Avoid ambiguity. (viii) Be brief (avoid unnecessary prolixity). (ix) Be orderly. Grice's claim is that we assume that speakers are following these maxims in their conversations. Appearing to flout them is the signal that the speaker's meaning is to be implied from the literal meaning of their utterances.

10 See Winer (1971, p. 11).

11 For a good survey of recent work see Part V of Evans (2012).

12 See Suarez (1994, pp. 5–10) for an extended discussion.

13 For example, if I observe water turning from a liquid to a solid as I freeze it, do I see the water *having* to solidify, or do I merely see it *happening* to solidify? Hume's claim is that we do not see it *having* to solidify.

14 Sticking with the example from the previous note, Hume's point is that while it would be surprising if the lowered temperature was not followed by the water solidifying, there is nonetheless no logical contradiction in the proposition 'The temperature was lowered to 0 °C at sea level and the water did not solidify' or 'The ambient temperature was above 0 °C at sea level and the water solidified'.

15 The other main challenge is what to make of theoretical terms for unobservable entities.

16 Keynes (2010, p. 380).

17 According to the frequency theory of probability, the probability of an outcome (of all *A*s turning out to be *B*s, say) equals the number of times *A*s have been observed to be *B*s divided by the number of observed *A*s. The idea is that the probability of *all A*s being *B*s is equal to the proportional frequency of *A*s being *B*s in the sample. Now a Hume would say that this is just to assume that the population as a whole will resemble the sample, which is precisely what he says logic cannot guarantee. But we can accept this logical point with equanimity if we trade on Aristotelian metaphysical principles.

Chapter three

1 See Grice (1986, p. 66).

2 See Hobbes (2016, chapter 46) and Mackie (1976, p. 86) for just two expressions of this widespread view. This impression is all the harder to remove for the comments of historians to the effect that the Church was 'the first totalitarian state' (Coulton, 1947, p. 458).

3 One of Hobbes's allegations against the scholastics (*Leviathan*, IV, chapter 46, p. 696).

4 Pieper attributes the infamous dryness of scholastic texts to this scholarly aspect of the project:

> If both the pagan and the Christian heritage of the ancient world were to be truly incorporated, ordering of the existing material undoubtedly came first and foremost. Moreover, that material had to be ordered in terms of being made accessible to teaching and learning. Inevitably, then, the wholly prosaic work of organising, sorting and classifying acquired a hitherto unknown importance. And quite naturally the writings of medieval scholasticism lacked the magic of personal immediacy. ... The dissolution of antiquity's world order was indeed taking place during these centuries. And if the major historical task was to acquire the riches of tradition, scholasticism could not but smack of the schoolroom. (1960, pp. 20, 23–4)

5 See Rosemann (2004, p. 11).

6 Good examples of important medieval figures who were not scholastics include John Scotus Eriugena, the Cathari and Albigensians, Bernard of Tours, Amalic of Bene, Joachim de Floris, Witelo, Theoderic of Freiburg, Raymond Lully, Roger Marston, Meister Eckhart, Raymond of Sabunde and Nicholas of Cusa. Eriugena is probably the most significant as his work is echoed down the centuries by various others who were attracted to his claim that there is only one entity, God, from which everything else is a never entirely distinct emanation. These non-scholastic thinkers tended to find the neo-Platonism of a Proclus or Plotinus attractive, while others were drawn to the epicureans and Lucretius. One also finds distinctly un-Aristotelian theses recurring in the works of these non-scholastic thinkers, theses like the transmigration of souls, pantheism, atheism, and the idea that God himself thinks in man.

7 Abelard's *Sic et Non* (Yes and No) is a collection of 158 theological questions (Abelard, 2012). The text itself is largely devoted to

cataloguing the contradictory answers to these questions to be found amongst the recognized authorities. Far from merely accepting what authorities had to say about important matters – a charge often laid against the scholastics – their point of departure is the explicit recognition that the authorities contradict themselves, and that it is impossible to accept any of them at face value.

8 *On Being and Essence*, Prologue. As in so many things, Aquinas is here following Aristotle, who insisted that 'the least initial deviation from the truth is multiplied later a thousandfold' (*On the Heavens*, book I, chapter 4, 271b9–10).

9 For very useful studies see Gilson (1925), William (1978, chapter 2), Cottingham (1986, chapter 2), Wilson (1991, chapter 1) and Sorell (1996, chapters 3 and 8). Spinoza's *Principles of Cartesian Philosophy* is also invaluable as a resource regarding how Descartes was understood by a philosophically sophisticated contemporary (Spinoza, 1998).

10 It is worth noting that these rules have often been criticized for being less than helpful. Williams repeats Leibniz's dismissive remark that the rules were 'like the precepts of some chemist; take what you need and do what you should, and you will get what you want' (Williams, 1978, p. 32). There is nothing wrong with the rules per se, implies Leibniz; it is just that they do not get one very far. Williams comes to Descartes's defence after conceding Leibniz's basic point by claiming that no abstract account of a method could possibly be truly informative in the absence of concrete problems. It is only when applied to a concrete problem, says Williams, that one can give content to the maxims (Williams, 1978, p. 33). Williams's point is well taken, for it explains the fact that purely abstract accounts of a method usually leave one with the impression that something important has been overlooked. But for our present purposes it is important to note that, concrete content or not, Descartes's rules are sufficient in and of themselves to mark a clear and unambiguous contrast with Aristotle. Moreover, Aristotle would not have dismissed the rules as simply unhelpful; they would have been dismissed as entirely wrong-headed.

11 Descartes does rather coyly suggest that he is not recommending this method for general use, and indeed that he would not advise everyone to use it. But these remarks seem to be aimed at those 'meddlesome and restless' characters who might want to apply Descartes's revisionary plans in the political sphere. The clear implication is that his method ought to be employed by philosophers.

12 See Boulter (2002, pp. 67–86; 2011, 617–41).

13 In his *Second Letter to Bernard*, Nicholas argues that if one accepts the condemnations of 1277, then we must say that Aristotle had certain knowledge of nothing other than his own soul. Nor can anyone else know anything of interest via purely natural means. Here we arrive at a form of scepticism Descartes would recognize. Nicholas argues as follows:

1. We can be sure that contradictories cannot be simultaneously true.
2. Every certitude 'resolves into this principle'. Anything that does not involve a logical contradiction is possible.
3. A contradiction is an affirmation and negation of the same thing.
4. Certitude in this sense is 'unqualified', that is, absolute.
5. Certitude of evidence has no degrees.
6. Except for the certitude of the faith, this is the only type of certitude.
7. All syllogisms reduce to the principle of non-contradiction (because to affirm the premises while denying the conclusion entails a logical contradiction).
8. *All inferences that are certain involve the identity of the antecedent and the consequent.*

(Why? If they are not identical, they are distinct, and so the state of affairs indicated by the antecedent can obtain without those indicated by the consequent and vice versa, for no logical contradiction arises when assuming that these circumstances obtain; so the premises do not entail the conclusion with the certainty that reduces to the first principle unless they are identical.)

9. Increase the chain of inferences as much as you like, if they are certain, then the first antecedent is identical to the last consequent.
10. So from the existence of A one cannot infer the existence of B with the certitude of the first principle (because A and B are not identical but distinct things). So Aristotle (or anyone else for that matter) never had certain knowledge of anything *other than his own soul.*

(Why? Because everything else Aristotle is acquainted with he knows via the senses. And sense experiences are *distinct* from the objects in the world which *cause* those experiences. As Ockham points out, because it is logically possible for us to be seeing a tree without that experience being caused by a tree, we cannot infer the existence of *anything* beyond our sense experiences.)

11 So Aristotle had no certainty of anything in natural philosophy or metaphysics (all such 'knowledge' begins in sense experience).

12 He had no probable knowledge either.

13 From this we can infer that, for post-1277 philosophy, the only certainties beyond the principle of non-contradiction are the certainties of the faith.

14 See Boulter (2011) for details.

15 I cannot resist making a further point about this meta-philosophy and its contemporary relevance. As noted in this chapter scholasticism was born out of the fall of the Roman Empire and the attempt to sift through the wreckage in a kind of salvage operation. Today we are faced with a similar problem. Newspapers from various parts of the world, such as *The Washington Post*, *The Financial Times*, *Der Spiegel* and *The Hindu*, have all recently mused on the end of the West as we know it. Although the crash of 2008, the decision of the United Kingdom to leave the European Union and the election of Trump to the presidency of the United States, do not come close to the cataclysm that was the fall of the Roman Empire, there is a sense in which we, like the scholastics, are picking through the wreckage of an Old World Order. What to salvage and what to jettison? That is the question. We need the right methodology for this task.

Chapter four

1 Gutting (2009, p. 2).

2 Gutting (2009).

3 He gives the following example: 'Even those who do not accept Kripke's overall account of reference and necessity can appreciate and appropriate his use of rigid designation to distinguish naming from description' (Ibid., p. 4).

4 For example, there is no entry for 'distinctions' in *A Dictionary of Philosophy* (Flew, 1975). Nor is there such an entry in the most recent *Oxford Dictionary of Philosophy*.

5 So, for example, a text's literal meaning might be about the parting of the Red Sea as Moses led the Israelites out of Egypt, but the parting of the Red Sea might itself have a spiritual meaning, perhaps foreshadowing baptism as it came to be understood in the New Testament.

6 For those new to Aristotle, one can consult the entries on 'one', 'identity' and 'difference' in Book V of Aristotle's *Metaphysics*, chapters VI and IX in particular. There Aristotle sets out what it is to be one per se and one *per accidens*; he distinguishes between *accidental* identity and identity per se, and all of these distinctions are correlated with various sense of 'difference'.

7 On this all were agreed. Aquinas is most emphatic: 'There is neither composition of quantitative parts in God, since He is not a body; nor composition of form and matter; nor does His nature differ from his suppositum; nor his essence from his being; neither is there in Him composition of genus and difference, nor of subject and accident. Therefore it is clear that God is in no way composite, but is altogether simple' (*Summa Theologiae*, I.I., q. 3, a. 7).

8 If X is identical to Y, and Z is identical to Y, then X is identical to Z. This rule is contravened by the Trinity inasmuch as the Father is identical to God, the Son is identical to God, but the Father is not identical to the Son.

9 The term 'healthy' applies in the first instance to organisms and provides the focal sense of the term. But the *causes* of health in organisms can be called healthy, as can the *indications* of health in organisms. These analogical senses are tightly connected to the original focal sense without being identical.

10 For a more complete appreciation of Aquinas on the application of terms to God one should consult *Super I Sententiarum*, 2.1.3 'How we know one simple God by many concepts', and *Summa Theologiae*, I.I., q. 13.

11 The line of reasoning behind this claim is not difficult to appreciate. Essentially Scotus says that analogy is just another form of equivocation, and so we cannot use terms with analogous senses in arguments that seek to establish conclusions about the nature or properties of God. Consider the following argument by way of illustration: this urine sample is healthy; health is a property of organisms; therefore this urine sample is a property of organisms. 'Health' is being used in analogically related senses in the premises. In this case the premises lead to a false conclusion, but Scotus's point is that the argument fails because of the fallacy of equivocation.

12 Scotus focuses on the concept of 'being' in particular to establish that there is a unified notion of being that applies to both God and creatures. Scotus is a difficult read, but for those who might be interested to follow this up a good place to start is his *Ordinatio*, I, d. 3, pars I, qq. 1–3.

13 I will focus here on the so-called 'positive' distinctions in real things, setting aside here the so-called 'negative distinctions' drawn between non-real beings or privations. That is, I will ignore for now distinctions like those drawn between Sherlock Holmes and Hercule Poirot (non-real beings) or between darkness and blindness (privations).

14 An extrinsic denomination is a referring expression which picks out a referent in virtue of one of the referent's extrinsic properties, for example, 'my old colleague'.

15 See his *Ordinatio*, I, d. ii, q. 3.

16 Set aside for now any difficulties we might have with his example given current physics.

17 It is worth distinguishing four positions on the matter of the relationship between the logical and real orders. Firstly, for those who deny that there is any omnipotent being, there is no guarantee that what is possible in the order of ideas is also possible in the real order (Aristotle). For those who maintain that there is an omnipotent being, historically there have been two main positions: (i) those who maintain that if *X* is logically possible then it is possible in the real order, but we can seldom be sure that *X* is logically possible without evidence from the real order, that is, actuality (Aquinas, Suarez); (ii) if *X* is logically possible then it is possible in the real order, and we can use the conceivability principle as a guide to logical possibility because God can do anything we can clearly and distinctly perceive (Descartes). Finally, there is the position of Hume, which implicitly or explicitly denies that there is an omnipotent being, but still maintains that if *X* is logically possible then *X* is possible in the real order, *and* that conceivability is a good guide to logical possibility.

18 I follow Braddon-Mitchell and Jackson's presentation of the argument. See Braddon-Mitchell and Jackson (2007, pp. 123–4).

19 Miller (2003, pp. 13–14).

Chapter five

1 Space considerations make it impossible to do justice to all of the arguments the scholastic entertained. I focus here on two arguments that are of enduring interest.

2 It was recognized, for example, that further arguments were required to establish that there is only one entity that is ontologically

fundamental, that this entity is simple, that this entity is infinite in power or that this entity has an intellect and will. This is important because one often sees the objection raised against the first three ways of Aquinas, for example, that even if they were sound they would not establish the existence of just one God, but are consistent with there being many Gods. See Edwards (2000, p. 203) as a typical example. The scholastics were perfectly aware of this and would routinely go on to offer further arguments as to why there can only be one occupant of this particular ontological category.

3 See chapter 39 of Aquinas's *Summa Contra Gentiles III*, entitled 'That Man's Happiness Does Not Consist in the Knowledge of God Acquired by Demonstration'.

4 Shaffer's motivation for denying (b) is particularly significant for scholastic neo-Aristotelians. He believes that denying (b) is the only way to avoid (c). Shaffer baulks at (c) because it entails the denial of full reality to the middle-sized composite bodies of common sense.

5 See Oppy (2012, pp. 687–704, 702).

6 Oppy (2012, p. 701).

7 Oppy (2012, p. 700).

8 See Vorobej (2006, p. 47).

9 Vorobej (2006, pp. 49–53).

10 See Hamblin (1970).

11 My source of the Quinean account is Roland (2014, pp. 43–61).

12 Not all Quineans agree. Anthony and Jenkins think naturalism can accommodate the a priori.

13 Quineans are not usually worried about making the distinction between the traditional reading of Hume and the so-called 'New Hume'. Most Quinean naturalists are traditional Humeans. However, some do accept full-blown efficient causal realism, for example, Kornblith and Boyd.

14 On this important point see Aristotle's *Metaphysics*, book II, chapter 2.

15 This distinction is not always recognized, but Richard P. Phillips drew attention to it in his *Modern Thomistic Philosophy*, Vol. II (Phillips, 1935, pp. 284–5). It is also recognized by Yandell (2005, pp. 185–6), who carefully distinguishes *chronological* from *concurrent* causes.

16 Remember that Aquinas maintains that it is impossible to disprove the eternity of the world on purely philosophical grounds.

17 As Henry of Ghent does, or a Kant.

18 For the uninitiated consider this famous sentence from Chomsky: 'Green ideas sleep furiously.' Chomsky's point is that we all appreciate that the sentence is grammatical while being nonsensical. It is nonsensical because it contains category mistakes. Ideas are not the sorts of things that can be coloured, so ideas cannot be green. And ideas are not the sort of thing that can sleep or be awake. And sleeping states are not the sorts of things that can be furious. As Wittgenstein would say, statements that contain category mistakes are 'not even false'.

19 And not only for Aristotle. One often hears the dictum, 'There are no vague things, only vague concepts.' Gareth Evans goes further than many by providing a deductive proof for the denial of vague entities in 'Can There Be Vague Objects?' found in Kim, Korman and Sosa (2012, p. 158). However, the relevance of vagueness for arguments for the existence of God is seldom noticed.

20 For those with Quine's question in mind about the number of possible men in a doorway, the answer is that there is no definite number of possible men to be found there precisely because they are merely possible. For those wondering about the application of the predicate 'infinite' to God, the ultimate actuality, there are issues as to whether the term is being applied univocally in this case. Reasons for doubting univocity here is that Suarez explicitly says that the 'infinite' in 'infinite being' is equivalent to 'being by itself' (as opposed to 'being from another'), 'existing necessarily' (as opposed to 'existing contingently'), 'being by essence' (as opposed to being by 'participation'), 'uncreated' (as opposed to 'created'). These are not the focal senses of 'infinite' as literally without end or boundary. See Suarez (2004, pp. 4, 6, 10–12).

21 See, for example, Aquinas, *Summa Theol.* Prima Pars, q. 2, art. 1, *ad secundum.*

Chapter six

1 But arguably since the outbreak of the First World War.

2 At the time of writing the most obvious examples are Brexit in the UK, Trump's election victory in the United States, Matteo Renzi's loss in Italy, the rise of Marine Le Pen in France, Viktor Orban in Hungary and Jeremy Corbyn in the UK.

3 This is part of the so-called 'Washington Consensus'. There have always been dissenting voices, at least within academe, but at least

since the end of the Second World War the predominant feeling and 'official' opinion within governments in the Western world has been in favour of liberalizing international trade. This was given institutional form in 1948 with the *General Agreement on Tariffs and Trade* and then again in 1995 with the *World Trade Organisation*. Current anti-immigration sentiment runs counter to the free movement of labour; anti-outsourcing sentiment runs counter to the free movement of capital; and the desire to protect 'home' industries from competition runs counter to the free movement of goods.

4 These are amongst the most pressing questions of our times. And the world is watching. The Russians and the Chinese in particular, whose social orders run on significantly different lines, are waiting to see just how resilient the West will prove to be, and what the West will become in the next few decades.

5 Of course the cynical will think this approach wrong-headed. They maintain that one arrives at policy proposals based on one's interests first, and then one goes in search of arguments to support them. This might be the psychological reality of policy makers, but it does not affect the point at issue in a fundamental way. At issue is that facts cannot support value-laden conclusions, regardless of the order of discovery.

6 Trump is the best example of this. Like most politicians he made many campaign promises he had no intention of keeping. What was new in this case was that his supporters were perfectly aware of this fact and supported him anyway. As the saying went, they took Trump 'seriously but not literally'. His campaign promises were exercises in value signalling, and not intended as genuine proposals, and his supporters knew this.

7 But see chapter 1 of Bell (2015) for a rebuttal of this claim. There he outlines four moral failings of the principle of one person one vote.

8 To get a sense of the depths of current disenchantment, consider these lines from James Mill (Bentham's pupil and father to John Stuart Mill): 'Every man possessed of reason is accustomed to weigh evidence and to be guided and determined by its preponderance. When various conclusions are, with their evidence, presented with equal care and with equal skill, *there is a moral certainty*, though some few may be misguided, *that the greatest number will judge right*, and that the greatest force of evidence, whatever it is, will produce the greatest impression' ('The Liberty of the Press', found in E. H. Carr's *The Twenty Years' Crisis: 1919–1939* (Carr, 2001, pp. 26–7), emphasis added). Do we believe such things now?

9 This is a summary of the reaction to Moore's Open Question Argument. Although Moore himself was a non-naturalist realist, his work did much to embolden anti-realism in meta-ethics.

10 This 'argument from queerness' can be traced back to Hume. It plays a prominent role in Mackie's *Ethics: Inventing Right and Wrong* (Mackie, 1977, pp. 38–42), and is at the centre of ongoing debates between internalists and externalists regarding the nature of moral motivation.

11 It is important to remember that, for Aquinas, 'human law does not derive from divine law but from natural law which is accessible through the employment of "right reason"' (Alves and Moreira, 2013, p. 30). For those wondering whether the natural law theory can be divorced from a Christian theological context, it is worth remembering both that Aristotle and the Stoics are usually seen as the originators of the natural law tradition, and that the Chinese developed their own version of the natural law theory that lacks any theological foundation (see Arthur Waldron, 2012, pp. 38–64). I take this to imply that while the natural law tradition certainly can be accommodated within a theological context, it need not be. Grotius suggests as much, writing that natural law would be valid 'even if we were to suppose ... that God does not exist or is not concerned with human affairs', and that 'the Law of Nature is so unalterable that it cannot be changed even by God himself' (p. 22). This view was echoed a century later by Emer de Vattel (2008, p. 69), the most influential natural law theorist of the eighteenth century: 'By studying the nature of things, and that of man in particular, we may thence deduce the rules which man must follow in order to attain his great end – to obtain the most perfect happiness of which he is susceptible. We call these rules the natural laws, or the laws of nature. They are certain ... independently of every consideration than that of his nature, and even though we should suppose him totally ignorant of the existence of God.'

12 Thomas Aquinas, *Summa Contra Gentiles*, Book III, ch. 113.

13 Education is necessary because, while these goods are usually provided for one in infancy and adolescence, eventually we all need to be able to secure them by one's own efforts. Education is vital to achieving this capacity.

14 This account sticks very closely to Aquinas's natural law theory, but leans heavily on Murphy (2001).

15 Here is Aquinas on the identification of right and reasonableness: 'Now in human actions, good and evil are predicated in relation to the reason, because ... the good of man is to be in accordance with reason, and evil is to be against reason' (*Summa Theologiae*, I–II, q. 18, a. 5).

16 This is the principle of synderesis in the terminology of traditional natural law theory. Here the 'reasons' in question are justificatory not motivational.

17 Again, in the terminology of traditional natural law theory, one would say that the good or the virtuous is that which is 'conducive to well-living' – utilitas ad bene vivendum (Aquinas, *Summa Theologiae*, I–II, q. 94, a. 3).

18 Examples of plausible kinds include those correlated with Ross's *prima facie* duties: duties of fidelity, reparation, gratitude, beneficence, justice (Ross, 2002).

19 On the importance of circumstances, see Aquinas (*Summa Theologiae*, I–II, q. 18, a. 3). This is essentially Aristotle's point that an action is right if it is done at the right time, to the right extent, by the right person, to the right people, in the right way, with the right implements and so forth.

20 That is, it is not enough to act so as to bring about a good end; one's primary motive must have been to bring about that end.

21 Aquinas writes, 'Nothing hinders an action that is good in one of the ways mentioned above from lacking goodness in another way. And thus it may happen that an action which is good in its species or in its circumstances is ordained to an evil end, or vice versa. However, an action is not good absolutely, unless it is good in all those ways; for evil results from any single defect' (*Summa Theologiae*, I–II, q. 18, a. 4).

22 Such a hierarchy is necessary because there is no ultimate harmony of interests that allows one to say that whenever an action is good for one person it will also be good for everyone concerned. When such clashes arise an ordering of goods is needed. A traditional ordering of goods is the following. Things are subordinated to persons; the useful and pleasurable are subordinated to necessary goods; the less urgent is subordinated to the more urgent; social goods are subordinated to necessary personal goods; civic goods are subordinated to necessary family goods; but private advantage is subordinated to the common good. These are usually taken to order goods that might be at issue between individuals and the social order of which they are members. But these principles might also be taken to apply to the ordering of goods at issue between individual nations and the international community at large.

23 That human nature is universal follows from our identification of that nature with our form. For more information on the nature of this form that takes its point of departure from developmental biology, see Raff (1996), West-Eberhard (2003) and Boulter (2002).

24 It is important to emphasize that this is *not* a form of consequentialism, and Aquinas is no utilitarian. He writes, 'The goodness of an action is not caused by the goodness of its effect, even though an action is said to be good from the fact that it can produce a good effect' (*Summa Theologiae*, I–II, q. 18, a. 2 and 3).

25 James Alvey (1999) writes, 'There are two major reasons why economics has become detached from moral concerns. First, the natural sciences came to be seen as successful, and the attempt was made to emulate that success in economics by applying natural science methods, including mathematics, to economic phenomena. Second, the self-styled economic science came to adopt positivism, which ruled out moral issues from science. itself.' Both the mathematization of economics and the adoption of positivism have proved highly problematic.

26 Utilitarianism and various forms of consequentialism have been popular in economic circles ever since Bentham. However, its shortcomings have always been more than readily apparent. See Boulter (2017) for a detailed explanation of the metaphysical difficulties in particular of consequentialism.

27 For recent efforts in this direction see Gregg and James (2012).

28 Speaking of the late Spanish scholastics, Schumpeter (1954, p. 97) writes, 'It is within their systems of moral theology and law that economics gained definite if not separate existence, and it is they who come nearer than does any other group to having been the 'founders' of scientific economics.' For further discussion see chapter 2 of Alves and Moreira, *The Salamanca School*. For extended studies see Grice-Hutchinson (1952, 1978).

29 For a good discussion of this see Smith (2012). See also Paul Oslington (2011).

30 The key value of Eucken's ordoliberalism is human dignity, and this shows in Eucken's focal research question: 'How can a modern industrialised economy and society be organised in a humane and efficient way?' (Eucken, 1951). For good introductions to Eucken see van Suntum et al. (2011, pp. 21–42). For an extended study of ordoliberalism as a whole see Bonefeld (2017).

31 This means that we can say that it is true that there is no *logical* connection between the empirical claim 'X is an aspect of human flourishing' and the value claim 'X is a good providing a reason for action'. But this logical point does not preclude the possibility that the truth conditions of both claims are identical, meaning that when the empirical claim is true, so too is the value claim. It is enough then

to establish objectively that X is a precondition of human health (adequate nutrition, say) to be able to claim that X is a good to be pursued.

32 One might advert to evolutionary psychology at this point and consider the possibility that the human mind is equipped with a 'moral module' that reliably produces certain responses to social circumstances. Such a module would account for the authority of the moral imperative.

33 See Anscombe (1981) [1958].

34 This is one of the 'take-aways' from Davidson (2001).

35 See Haight (1980) for a penetrating look at how we so often let ourselves down in this respect.

36 If one remembers that the relationship between (i) states of affairs, (ii) what one *thinks* about these states of affairs and (iii) what one *says* about these states of affairs is anything but straightforward when one's interests are involved, then expressions of disagreement will not strike us as particularly significant from a meta-ethical point of view.

EPILOGUE

As mentioned in the Preface, this is an unusual book on medieval philosophy. While there are many introductions to medieval philosophy, introductions to particular medieval figures, and many specialist works on all aspects of medieval philosophy, there are very few book-length efforts to explain to non-specialists why medieval philosophy matters. That has been my task here. Being forced to think about why my academic interests should be taken seriously by those who do not happen to share my obsession has been a very useful exercise. Explaining oneself to a non-specialist audience encourages one to see old material in new ways.

The results of this new orientation can be stated summarily as follows.

There are pressing questions the sciences cannot address. These questions are not confined to spiritual or religious matters. Many arise in the context of the sciences themselves, and many more have their origin in the tensions to be found between the various domains of our social order. The import of these questions extends well beyond the halls of academe. This means that the redundancy thesis, that is, the view that there are no important questions that cannot be settled by the sciences, is false. This reopens the possibility that there might very well be a philosophy that can matter to society at large. A philosophy that matters would be a philosophy that can address precisely these sorts of problems in a compelling fashion.

These philosophical problems are aporetic in nature. They arise when we notice that there are tensions between lines of thought and principles of practical rationality that are compelling when considered in isolation but fail to add up to a coherent whole. The task of philosophizing per se is to restore consistency. The mark of philosophical success is to remove these tensions while respecting both common sense and the sciences. Failure to respect common sense and the sciences casts a philosopher out of the garden of ordinary experience and into irrelevancy.

The scholastics solve two classic aporia, that is, the problem of universals and the problem of change, in a manner consistent with common sense while laying the ground work for the very possibility of the sciences themselves. Central to these efforts are the doctrines of hylomorphism and essentialism. Both doctrines are central to any philosophy that can matter to society at large.

The scholastic framework not only provides the metaphysical background against which the sciences become possible. This framework also provides the background necessary for scientific experimentation itself by motivating both the aim of experimentation (identifying causal relations) and the means (the rules of good experiment design). The key doctrines here were causal realism and the notions of powers and liabilities. Both doctrines are central to any philosophy that can matter to society at large. The relevance of the scholastic framework was made particularly clear by contrasting it with both Hume and Kant.

The reason the scholastic framework is able to engage with both common sense and the sciences is that its meta-philosophy, its philosophy of philosophy, is very different from that of Descartes, whose views on these matters decisively changed philosophy's self-image. The scholastics did *not* take the theologically motivated epistemological turn of early modernity. Unlike Descartes, they do not make the quest for self-evident and certain foundations the starting point of philosophical reflection. Because defeating the radical sceptic is not the mark of philosophical success, the scholastic is free to remain in, or rejoin, the real world of pre-theoretical experience. In one of the great historical ironies, the roots of Cartesianism lie in theological concerns of the late thirteenth century and the condemnations of 1277.

Solving aporia is largely a matter of drawing distinctions. Philosophers today are familiar with the need for conceptual distinctions in order to avoid confused thinking. But the scholastics developed an armoury of distinctions to be drawn between things in the real order. For reasons relating to the condemnations of 1277, post-Cartesian philosophers have a tendency to conflate distinctions in the realm of ideas with distinctions in the real order. This has led to a number of serious metaphysical errors. Recovering the scholastic material on real distinctions allows us to avoid these errors, perhaps the most important of which from a societal point of view has been the alleged 'naturalistic fallacy' associated with Moore's Open Question Argument.

Readmitting the scholastics to the circle of philosophical colleagues is made easier when we recognize that the scholastics were not the dogmatic theologians they are often made out to be. Their work begins with explicit and frank accounts of the contradictions to be found amongst recognized authorities on doctrinal matters. Their philosophical *bona fides* are perhaps best illustrated where we would least expect it, in arguments for the existence of God. When these arguments are properly understood, it becomes clear that the scholastic theologians were providing rational grounds for the existence of a fundamental level of reality. As it happens, this ontological claim is upheld by most post-Cartesian philosophy and the sciences, but it is rarely well supported. When the traditional arguments for the existence of God are seen in this light it becomes obvious that secular thinkers should be able to appreciate this scholastic achievement.

But perhaps the most important feature of the scholastic framework is the following: the aporia that beset our social order have their deepest root in the fact that we have severed our cognitive authority (the sciences) from our political and economic images and principles. The naturalistic fallacy, along with the fact–value, is–ought gap, has led many to believe that the sciences, however competent they may be in the empirical realm, cannot speak to values. This has led to Weberian 'disenchantment', and the belief that our best factual information cannot be brought to bear on matters political and economic. We are left rudderless when trying to cope with the myriad contradictions and tensions of our social order. The scholastic framework matters because it restores the head to the body of the social order. Overcoming the naturalistic fallacy allows for the possibility of 'legitimacy' in the social realm. Much work still needs to be done, but scholastic principles of practical reasoning, themselves embedded in the metaphysical doctrines explored in this book, provide the framework for serious reflection on our society's ills. No philosophy could matter more.

SOME USEFUL LATIN TERMS AND PHRASES FOR PHILOSOPHERS

Contemporary philosophy betrays much of its medieval past by its continued use of the technical terminology of the scholastics. Often the original meaning of the medieval Latin has been maintained, but not always. The following is a list of useful Latin terms and phrases.

A fortiori	From the stronger
A parte rei	In reality
A posteriori	From the latter (e.g. one reasons a posteriori when one reasons from effects, or from what is ontologically dependant, to causes)
A priori	From the former (e.g. one reasons a priori when one reasons from causes, or from what is ontological independent, to effects)
Ad/ab absurdum	To/from absurdity
Ab aeterno	From eternity
Ab initio	From the beginning
Actiones secundum fidei	Actions follow belief
Ad hominem	To the man
Ad infinitum	To infinity
Ad nauseam	To seasickness
Adaequatio intellectus et rei	Adequation of intellect and thing (truth)

Addendum	Something added at the end of a work
Adversus solem ne loquitor	Don't speak against the sun (don't defend the obviously false)
Agere sequitur esse	Action follows being (an entity's mode of being and nature determine how it can act)
Audi alteram partem	Hear the other side
Bibo ergo sum	I drink therefore I am
Bona fide	In good faith, sincerely
Ceteris paribus	Everything else being equal
Compos mentis	Of sound mind
Condemnant (damnant) quod non intellegunt	They condemn (damn) what they don't understand
Contra principia negantem non est disputandum	Do not argue with someone who does not accept any common premises
Credo quia absurdum est	Tertullian's sense is that some items of faith would never suggest themselves to unaided reason; it would have to be a matter of faith rather than reason
Cum hoc ergo propter hoc	With this, so because of this
De omnibus dubitandum	Doubt everything
De re/de dicto	Of the thing/of the thing said. Modal propositions are often ambiguous. Consider: 'Every *A* could be *B*'. This might mean 'Of anything it is the case that if it is *A* it could be *B*' (de re). Or it might mean 'It is true that "Every *A* could be *B*"' (de dicto)
Demonstratio	Reasoning from self-evident premises
Dialectica	Reasoning from probable premises
Distinctio ex natura rei	A real distinction as opposed to a modal, formal or mental distinction
Docendo disco, scribendo cogito	I learn by teaching, I think by writing

Ens	Being, a being
Ens per se/per accidens	Substances as opposed to accidents; effects that follow naturally from their causes versus those that follow by chance; being unified per se versus being unified by accident (an aggregate)
Ens rationis	A being of reason (negations, privations, relations of reason) as opposed to a being in the natural order
Ens reale	A being in the natural order
Entia non sunt multiplicanda praetor necessitate	Entities are not to be added without necessity
Entitas ipse involuit aptitudinem ad extorquendum certum assensum	Reality has a way of coercing consensus
Esse	To be, to exist, to be present
Et supposito nil point in esse	Saying it don't make it so
Ex hypothesi	By hypothesis
Ex nihilo nihil fit	Nothing comes from nothing
Exempli gration	For example, that is to say (e.g.)
Experimentum crucis	A crucial experiment
Fere libentur homines id quod volunt credunt	People believe what they want to believe
Fides quaerens intellectum	Faith seeking understanding
Flatus vocis	Breath of voice (mere noise)
Fundamentum	A foundation or basis, used in both the epistemological and the ontological senses
Genus	Birth, origin, offspring, kind, sort, class
Haecceitas	Thisness, bare particular

Homo unius libri temeo	I fear a man of one book
Hypotheses non fingo	I do not assert that any of my hypotheses are true (Newton)
In rerum natura	In the natural order
Infinitas	Infinite, endless, countless, indefinite, lack of determination and form
Ipsa scientia potestas est	Knowledge is power
Ipso facto	By the fact itself
Locus classicus	A classic source (of a point of view)
Magnus opus	A masterpiece
Malum in se	Wrong in itself
Malum prohibitum	Wrong because prohibited by law
Mea culpa	Through my fault
Mens sana in corpore sano	A healthy mind in a healthy body
Modus operandi	Method, way of working/operating
Modus ponens, tollens, morons	The method of placing, of removing, of the moron
Mundus vult decipi, ergo decipiatur	The world wants to be deceived, so let it be deceived
Mutatis mutandis	After changing what needs to be changed
Nanos gigantum humeris insidentes	Dwarfs standing on the shoulders of giants
Natura nihil frustra ficat	Nature does nothing in vain
Natura non facit saltus	Nature makes no leaps
Nemo saltat sobrius	No one dances sober
Nihil in intellectu nisi prius in sensu	There is nothing in the mind that is not first in the senses
Non liquet	Not proven, not evident

Non sequitur	It does not follow
Nosce te ipsum	Know thyself
Omnia dicta fortiori si dicta Latina	Everything sounds more impressive in Latin
Onus probandi	Burden of proof
Ordo	Order, norm, rule, nature. Of the prior to the posterior in perfection, nature, cause, time, place, height essentially or accidentally
Per	By, through, by means of
Per se	By means of itself, intrinsically
Per se nota	Self-evident, known through itself
Perfectio	To achieve, finish, complete, conclude
Petitio principia	To ask for what is at issue (begging the question)
Post hoc propter hoc	After this so because of this
Prima facie	At first appearances
Primum mobile/movens	First mover
Principia probant, non probantur	Principles prove; they are not to be proven
Qua definitione	By definition
Quidditas	Whatness, essence
Quod erat demonstrandum	That which is to be proved (QED)
Quod gratis asseritur, gratis negatur	What is asserted without reason can be denied without reason
Quod natura non dat Salmantica non praestat	The University of Salamanca cannot make up for nature's deficiencies
Quod supplantum, prius bene sciendus	Understand well what you would overturn or supplant

Ratio	Reason, cause, argument, nature, relation, principle, foundation, definition, order, notion, norm and so forth
Reductio ad absurdam	To reduce to absurdity
Repugnantia	Inconsistency, incompatibility, contradiction
Res	Thing
Salva veritate	With truth intact
Scientia	Demonstrative knowledge, science, skill
Sensu lato, stricto, plenior	In the wide/strict/fullest sense
Sic	Thus
Sic et non	Yes and no
Sine qua non	A necessary condition
Sui generis	Of its own kind
Tabula rasa	Blank or scraped slate
Tertium non datur	There is no third possibility (law of excluded middle)
Veritas	Truth
Videlicet	Namely, that is to say (viz.)
Viva voce	Oral examination
Vox populi, vox Dei	The voice of the people is the voice of God

APPENDIX I

When were the Middle Ages?

The period referred to by the term 'the Middle Ages' has never been entirely stable. It used to be standard to say that the Middle Ages range from 500 AD to 1500 AD, roughly from the fall of the Roman Empire to the Renaissance or Early Modernity. Most agree that the fall of the Roman Empire marks the beginning of a new historical period. But many now say early modernity started well before 1500. Conversely, others maintain that the Middle Ages did not end until after the French Revolution in 1789. The reason for the differing assessments stems from the fact that historical time periods are not natural kinds with clear divisions found in the very nature of things. Rather they are terms used by historians to impose some order on historical events which can otherwise look like 'just one damn thing after another'. Thus historical time periods usually reflect the interests and attitudes of the historian as much as the events themselves. Indeed, the terms 'medieval' and 'Middle Ages' tend to be used as terms of abuse. If an historian admires a thinker or artist, or if he finds an event laudable, then he tends to calls it 'modern' regardless of the date. If not, then he calls it 'medieval'. Although there are now many critics of modernity, it remains the case that the common perception of the Middle Ages amongst the general public was largely fixed by the champions of modernity and the detractors of the medieval. It is also important to bear in mind that the various elements of the social order do not change in lock-step. A development in politics may or may not be accompanied by a change, say, in the art world. This means that one and the same period may be 'modern' in one respect while remaining 'medieval' in another.

To avoid confusion, in this book I use the terms 'medieval' and 'scholastic' to refer to a particular philosophical project. A thinker counts as distinctly medieval not because of their dates but because of their commitment to this particular philosophical project. On this view, a twentieth-century figure could be 'medieval'. A philosopher is 'modern' in this philosophical sense if they reject this project.

I have also used the term 'modernity' to refer to a particular social order, one in which the sciences play the role of cognitive legitimizer, parliamentary democracy combined with constitutionalism is the favoured stance in the political realm and the reliance on open markets shapes our economy. This account is consistent with the characterization of modernity as the age of individualism, when thinking for oneself becomes the rallying cry, an age where self-expression, self-discovery and personal development are seen as moral rights, an age ready to accept change, desirous of the chance to explore, to experiment and to overthrow traditional ways of life. Now the central theme of this book is that a 'medieval' philosophical framework is best placed to tackle the inherent tensions in the social order of modernity. After all, this is the basis of my claim that medieval philosophy matters.

However, the fact remains that most 'medieval' thinkers (in our philosophical sense) lived during the so-called 'long Middle Ages' (in the politico-socio-historical sense). So it is worth having some idea of the shape of this period. The following is a collection of significant political, intellectual and cultural dates of the long Middle Ages:

Year/period	Event
354–476	Augustine and the fall of Rome. Augustine witnesses the collapse of the Roman Empire. He defends Christianity, which had been blamed for the fall of Rome (*City of God*). The last emperor, Romulus Augustus, dies in 476 and is not replaced. For some this marks the beginning of the so-called 'Dark Ages' – 'dark' because we have few written records from the period.
380	The Roman emperor Constantine makes Christianity the official religion of the Roman Empire. For some this marks the beginning of the Middle Ages.

Year/period	Event
700	The expansion of Islam. For some this marks the beginning of the Middle Ages.
719–41	Carolingian Renaissance: The first of many renaissances. End of the 'Dark Ages', beginning of the Middle Ages?
800	Coronation of Charlemagne: First emperor of the Holy Roman Empire. The boundaries of the Holy Roman Empire are the boundaries of the political-social-historical Middle Ages for some.
980–1037	Avicenna: One of the major Arabic commentators on Aristotle, and big influence on Aquinas.
1000–	The rise of towns and cities, and the birth of a new social animal – the intellectual (those who earn their keep by teaching), and the founding of universities begins: Bologna (1088); University of Paris (1215); Oxford and Padua (1228); Rome (1245); Salamanca (1250).
1033–1109	St Anselm (he of the *ontological argument*).
1073–85	Gregory VII and the 'Gregorian reforms'. The Church starts to become independent of secular authorities and the Holy Roman emperor. First signs of the split between Church and State – essential to modern Western political thought.
1079–1142	Peter Abelard (logician and theologian, ill-fated lover of Heloise).
1095	The First Crusade begins. The Second (1146–8); the Third (1188–92); the Fourth (1202–4); the Fifth (1217–21). Some smaller Crusades continued in the East into the sixteenth century.
1122	Concordat of Worms. The Investiture controversy. The Holy Roman Emperor no longer selects bishops and abbots. The battles of Pope versus Emperor become a staple of medieval political life.
1126–98	Averroes: A major Arabic commentator on Aristotle. Poster boy of the so-called 'Latin Averroists', Siger of Brabant and Boethius of Dacia of the late thirteenth century.
1135–1204	Maimonides (he of *Guide to the Perplexed*).

(Continued)

Year/period	Event
1213–44	Albigensian Crusade. A heretical group called the Cathars in the south of France is crushed. The struggle with heresy, around since the beginning of the organized Church, continues.
1215	*Magna Carta* written. This document is seminal in Western history because it expresses the principle that the rule of law applies to everyone, including kings and emperors.
Mid-1200s	All of Aristotle's works now available. Until now only some logical works of the *Organon* had been known. Now the metaphysics, ethics, politics and scientific works are read.
1225–74	Thomas Aquinas and the 'Golden Age' of Scholasticism in full bloom.
1231	First papal bull announcing the establishment of *The Inquisition* (charged with rooting out heresy). The teaching order called the Dominicans take lead role.
1265–1308	John Duns Scotus: Scotland's most influential scholastic thinker.
1265–1321	Dante (he of *The Divine Comedy*).
1277	Condemnation of 219 propositions by Etienne Tempier, bishop of Paris.
1285–1349	William of Ockham (he of 'the razor'): England's most influential scholastic thinker, who died of plague.
1300–after 1347	Nicolas of Autrecourt: Often called 'The Medieval Hume'.
1313–75	Boccaccio (he of *The Decameron*, in which a group of friends escapes from Florence and the plague and passes the time by telling stories).
1324	Marsilius of Padua writes *Defensor Pacis*, a highly influential work of political philosophy in which he argues that the laws of the land must be arrived at via a process involving all of the people (not just the emperor, Pope and nobles) and that the Pope should have no political authority whatsoever. First fully fleshed out expression of democratic principles.

Year/period	Event
1337–1453	*The Hundred Years War*. The Plantagenets (French rulers of England) begin their campaign to extent their domains onto the Continent, particularly French territory. Their high water mark was The Battle of Agincourt (1415), but the French eventually rally behind Joan of Arc. The end of this war marks the last occasion on which these islands mounted an aggressive campaign on the Continent (as opposed to addressing aggression started by Continental powers, that is, the Napoleonic wars, the Crimean war, the First World War and the Second World War).
1341	Petrarch becomes poet laureate. For some this marks the end of the Middle Ages.
1343–1400	Chaucer (he of *The Canterbury Tales*).
1347	First wave of the plague known as *The Black Death* (the one that got Ockham) wipes out 30–40 per cent of Europe. In today's terms it would be roughly equivalent to twenty-six million deaths in England alone. The cause was totally unknown. Seen as the end of civilization at the time. Our best guess now is that it was a combination of anthrax (from cattle) and bubonic plague (from fleas on rats).
1378–1417	*The Great Schism*. A Pope in Rome and another in Avignon! Incalculable damage done to the prestige of the Church.
1381	The Great Peasant's Revolt: One of the most significant and best documented of the peasant uprisings. The shocking decline in numbers due to plague destabilized labour relations. Peasants and new free labour were able to demand higher wages because there was a labour shortage. Nobles weren't too pleased.
1452–1519	Leonardo da Vince: The renaissance in full bloom.
1453	Constantinople taken by the Ottomans. Scholars fleeing Ottoman rule head west, and contribute to the Renaissance. This marks the end of the Middle Ages for some.
1455–89	*War of the Roses*: English civil war, fighting over which royal family will rule.
1468–1534	Cardinal Cajetan, begins the post-nominalist revival of Aquinas.

(Continued)

Year/period	Event
1473–1543	Copernicus: This polish man of the Church revolutionizes astronomy.
1492	Columbus sets out for America. For some this marks the end of the Middle Ages.
1509	Publication of Erasmus's *In Praise of Folly*.
1517	Luther starts the *Protestant Reformation*. Many see this as the end of the Middle Ages, the idea being that the Middle Ages are defined by the unchallenged authority of Catholicism. It is also seen as the real impetus behind the rise of individualism.
1525–1640	Spain's 'Golden Century' begins, coinciding with the rise of the School of Salamanca and the great 'Silver Age' of scholasticism. Vitoria, de Soto, Azpilcueta, Medina, Mercado, Molina, Mariana, Suarez: This stable of thinkers is *both* the vanguard of the Counter-Reformation *and* the trailblazers of modernity.
1525–94	Palestrina (Giovanni Pierluigi da) Renaissance composer of scared music. Pinnacle of polyphony.
1529	Siege of Vienna by the Ottomans.
1532	Francisco de Vitoria, founder of the School of Salamanca, delivers lectures collected under the title *Readings on the Indians and on the Law of War*. Building on Aquinas, Vitoria sets out the basic principles of international law, and argues against absolutism of state power.
1548–1617	Francisco Suarez: Author of the *Metaphysical Disputations* (a compendium of scholastic knowledge) and the most influential scholastic of the 'Silver Age'. This work was well known to Descartes's teachers at La Fleshe; it was fully digested by Leibniz, and influenced both Catholic and Protestant theologians.
1564–1642	Galileo Galilei. Defends Copernicus in his *Dialogue Concerning the Two Chief World Systems*. Clashes with the Catholic Church over his realism regarding astronomical systems (the Church was anti-realist vis-à-vis astronomy).
1564–1616	Shakespeare.

Year/period	Event
1588–1679	Thomas Hobbes: Founder of English moral and political philosophy.
1596–1650	Rene Descartes: Poster boy of the Early Modern period.
1618–48	*Thirty Years' War*: Fought largely in the heartland of the Holy Roman Empire, that is, on what would eventually become the territory of Austria and a united Germany under Bismarck. Appalling horrors suffered by the civilian populations. Brought to an end with the *Treaty of Westphalia*, which establishes the rules of international relations, rules not seriously challenged until the aftermath of the Second Gulf War in Iraq.
1625	Hugo Grotius's *The Rights of War and Peace: Including the Law of Nature and of Nations*. Building on the Salamanca School, Grotius outlines a vision of international law which was influential in the formulation of the *Treaty of Westphalia*.
1632–1704	John Locke. British empiricism begins.
1632–77	Spinoza. Cartesian rationalism continues.
1642–1727	Isaac Newton. A new physics with lasting impact.
1646–1716	Leibniz: Last canonical figure to be fully versed in scholastic thought (particularly Suarez)?
1686–1750	Johan Sebastien Bach: Pinnacle of Baroque music.
1688	*The Glorious Revolution*: England's much less bloody version of the French Revolution. A king who must respect a House of Parliament with elected representatives is established. End of the Middle Ages in England?
1711–76	David Hume. British empiricism continues.
1720s–on	*The Industrial Revolution* and the beginning of 'the great escape' from the Malthusian poverty trap. Arguably the most significant event in world history, and a real historical breach. Why it started in England and not somewhere else is one of the outstanding historical questions.
1724–1804	Kant. Hume and Newton reconciled by the 'Copernican Turn'.

(Continued)

Year/period	Event
1755	This year marks the publication of Richard Cantillon's *An Essay on Economic Theory*, written in 1730s, styled the 'cradle of political economy'.
1756–91	Wolfgang Amadeus Mozart: Principal figure of the golden age of classical music.
1770–1827	Ludwig van Beethoven: Pinnacle of classical music.
1775–83	*American 'Revolutionary' Wars* – a war of independence rather than a revolution. 'No taxation without representation!' *The Federalist Papers* and the American Constitution itself show how a people can rule itself without a king.
1776	Publication of Adam Smith's *The Wealth of Nations*.
1789	*French Revolution*. The first major Continental power to get rid of the monarchy (in any form). For some *this* marks the end of the Middle Ages.
1803–15	*Napoleonic wars*. The great trauma of the early nineteenth century. Castlereagh (British foreign minister) and Metternich (Austrian foreign minister) put Europe back together again. But tension gradually increases between the new revolutionary powers (Britain and France) and the old world monarchies of Austria, Prussia and Russia.
1806	Dissolution of the Holy Roman Empire by Napoleon (end of the political-social-historical Middle Ages by my lights).
1848	Revolutions in Western and Central Europe continue the democratic and anti-monarchist thrust of the French Revolution.
1867	The Reform Act in UK. The vote now extended to non-property owners.
1867	Publication of Karl Marx's *Das Capital*.
1871	Germany unified under Bismarck.
1905/The First World War	Austrian and German houses fall/Russian Revolution. The end of (effective) monarchy in Europe. Perhaps this is the end of the Middle Ages?
1918	Suffrage for all men and women of age in the UK.

BIBLIOGRAPHY

Alves, Andre Azevedo and Moreira, Jose (2013) *The Salamanca School.* New York: Bloomsbury.
Alvey, James (1999) "A Short History of Economics as a Moral Science," *Journal of Markets and Morality*, Vol. 2, No. 1, pp. 53–73.
Anscombe, Elizabeth (1981) [1958] "Modern Moral Philosophy" in *Collected Philosophical Papers*, Vol. III. Minneapolis: University of Minnesota Press, pp. 26–42.
Aquinas, Thomas (1945) *The Basic Writings of Saint Thomas Aquinas*, Vols 1–2. Pegis (ed.) New York: Random House.
Aristotle (1941) *The Basic Works of Aristotle*. McKeon (ed.) New York: Random House.
Aristotle (2004) *Metaphysics*. Translation by Lawson-Tancred. London: Penguin, p. xxiii.
Abelard, Peter (2012) *Sic et Non*. Nabu Press.
Bain, William (ed.) (2017) *Medieval Foundations of International Relations*. London: Routledge.
Bell, Daniel (2015) *The China Model*. Princeton: Princeton University Press.
Blumenberg, Hans (1987) *The Genesis of the Copernican World*. Cambridge, MA: MIT Press.
Bonefeld, Werner (2017) *The Strong State and the Free Economy*. London: Rowman & Littlefield.
Boulter, Stephen (2002) "Hume on Induction: Genuine Problem or Theology's Trojan Horse?" *Philosophy*, Vol. 77, No. 299, pp. 67–86.
Boulter, Stephen (2007) *The Rediscovery of Common Sense Philosophy*. Houndmills: Palgrave Macmillan.
Boulter, Stephen (2011) "The Medieval Origins of Conceivability Arguments," *Metaphilosophy*, Vol. 42, No. 5, pp. 617–41.
Boulter, Stephen (2012) "Can Evolutionary Biology Do Without Aristotelian Essentialism? " *Human Nature* (Royal Institute of Philosophy Supplement), Vol. 70, pp. 83–104.
Boulter, Stephen (2017) "Can Consequence Be Right-Makers?" *Philosophia*, pp. 1–21. Doi:10.1007/s11406-016-9757-0.
Braddon-Mitchell, David and Jackson, Frank (2007) *Philosophy of Mind and Cognition: An Introduction*. Oxford: Blackwell.

Butterfield, Herbert (1957) *The Origins of Modern Science, 1300–1800.* New York: Macmillan.
Cantor, Norman (2002) *In the Wake of the Plague: The Black Death and the World It Made*. London: Pocket Books.
Carr, Edward Hallett (2001) *The Twenty Years' Crisis, 1919–1939: An Introduction to the Study of International Relations*. Houndmills: Palgrave Macmillan.
Charles, David (2000) *Aristotle on Meaning and Essence*. Oxford: Oxford University Press.
Coulton, George Gordon (1947) *Medieval Panorama*. Macmillan, p. 458.
Lewis, David (1983) "Extrinsic Properties," *Philosophical Studies,* vol. 44, pp. 197–200.
Cottingham, John (1986) *Descartes*. Oxford: Blackwell.
Dales, Richard (1973) *The Scientific Achievement of the Middle Ages*. Philadelphia: University of Pennsylvania Press.
Davidson, Donald (2001) "On the Very Idea of a Conceptual Scheme" in *Inquiries into Truth and Interpretation*. Oxford: Oxford University Press, pp. 183–98.
Deneen, Patrick (2018) *Why Liberalism Failed*. New Haven: Yale University Press.
Descartes, Rene (1990) *The Philosophical Writings of Descartes*, Vols 1–2. Translations by Cottingham, Stoothoff and Murduch. Cambridge: Cambridge University Press.
DeLanda, Manuel (2015) *Philosophical Chemistry: Genealogy of a Scientific Field*. London: Bloomsbury.
Duhem, Pierre (1954) *Le Systeme du Monde*. Paris: Librairie Scientifique Hermann et Cie.
Duhem, Pierre (1955) *Etudes Sur Leonard de Vinci*, Vols 1–3. Paris: F. de Nobele Librairie.
Edwards, Paul (2000) "Objections to Cosmological Arguments" in *Philosophy of Religion: A Guide and Anthology*. Davies (ed.) Oxford: Oxford University Press.
Eucken, Walter (1951) *This Unsuccessful Age*. New York: Oxford University Press.
Evans, Gareth (2012) "Can There Be Vague Objects?" in *Metaphysics: An Anthology*. Kim, Korman and Sosa (eds). Oxford: Wiley-Blackwell.
Flew, Antony (editorial consultant) (1975) *A Dictionary of Philosophy*. London: Pan Books.
Galston, William (2018) *Anti-Pluralism: The Populist Threat to Liberal Democracy*. New Haven: Yale University Press.
Gellner, Ernest (1988) *Plow, Sword and Book: The Structure of Human History*. Chicago: University of Chicago Press.
Gilson, Etienne (1925) *Rene Descartes, Discours de la Methode: Texte et Commentaire*. Paris: Vrin.

Goff, Jacque le (2007) *The Birth of Europe*. Oxford: Blackwell.
Goldstein, Thomas (1995) *Dawn of Modern Science: From the Ancient Greeks to the Renaissance*. New York: Da Cap Press.
Gregg, Samuel and James, Harold (2012) *Natural Law, Economics, and the Common Good*. St Andrews Studies in Philosophy and Public Affairs. Exeter: Imprint.
Grice, Paul (1989) *Studies in the Way of Words*. Cambridge, MA: Harvard University Press.
Grice, Paul (1986) "Reply to Richards" in *Philosophical Grounds of Rationality: Intentions, Categories, Ends*. Grandy and Warner (eds). Oxford: Clarendon Press.
Grice-Hutchinson, Marjorie (1952) *The School of Salamanca: Readings in Spanish Monetary Theory, 1544–1605*. Oxford: Clarendon Press.
Grice-Hutchinson, Marjorie (1978) *Early Economic Thought in Spain, 1177–1740*. London: Allen & Unwin.
Grotius, Hugo *On the Rights of War and Peace*. Forgotten Books, p. 22.
Gutting, Gary (2009) *What Philosophers Know: Case Studies in Recent Analytic Philosophy*. Cambridge: Cambridge University Press.
Haight, Mary (1980) *A Study of Self-Deception*. New Jersey: Humanities Press.
Hamblin, Charles (1970) *Fallacies*. Newport News: Vale Press.
Hausman, Daniel M. (ed.) (2008) *The Philosophy of Economics: An Anthology*. Cambridge: Cambridge University Press.
Hawking, Stephen and Mlodinow, Leonard (2010) *The Grand Design*. New York: Bantam Books.
Hobbes, Thomas (2016) *Leviathan*. London: Penguin Classics.
Hooykaas, Reijer (1972) *Religion and the Rise of Modern Science*. Edinburgh: Scottish Academic Press.
Hume, David (1989) *A Treatise of Human Nature*, 2nd ed. Oxford: Clarendon Press.
Ilgmann (2011) "Walter Eucken's Principles of Economic Policy Today," CAWN Discussion Paper, no. 49.
Jaeger, Gregg (2017) "Quantum Potentiality Revisited," in *Philosophical Transactions. Series A: Mathematical, Physical and Engineering Sciences* Vol. 375, No. 2106.
Keynes, Maynard (2010) *A Treatise on Probability*. Wildside Press LLC.
Kim, Jaegwon, Korman, Daniel and Sosa, Ernest (eds) (2012) *Metaphysics: An Anthology*. Oxford: Wiley-Blackwell.
Koyre, Alexandre (1956) "The Origins of Modern Science," *Diogenes*, Vol. 4, No. 16, pp. 1–22.
Krastev, Ivan (2017) *After Europe*. Philadelphia: University of Pennsylvania Press.
Kuhn, Thomas (1974) *The Structure of Scientific Revolutions*. Chicago: University of Chicago Press.

Lessnoff, Michael (1999) *Political Philosophers of the Twentieth Century.* Oxford: Blackwell.
Lewis, David (1987, 2002) *A Survey of Metaphysics.* Oxford: Oxford University Press.
Lowe, Edward Jonathan (2001) *The Possibility of Metaphysics: Substance, Identity and Time.* Oxford: Clarendon Press.
Lowe, Edward Jonathan (2007) *The Four-Category Ontology: A Metaphysical Foundation for Natural Science.* Oxford: Oxford University Press.
Mackie, John Leslie (1976) *Problems from Locke.* Oxford: Clarendon Press.
Mackie, John Leslie (1977) *Ethics: Inventing Right and Wrong.* Harmondsworth: Penguin.
Marenbon, John (2016) *Medieval Philosophy: A Very Short Introduction.* Oxford: Oxford University Press.
Martin, Christopher (1988) *Philosophy of Thomas Aquinas.* London: Routledge.
Miller, Alex (2003) *An Introduction to Contemporary Metaethics.* Cambridge: Polity Press.
Mokyr, Joel (2009) *The Enlightened Economy: Britain and the Industrial Revolution 1700–1850.* London: Penguin.
Moore, George Edward (1965) *Some Main Problems of Philosophy.* New York: Macmillan.
Morgenthau, Hans (1993) *Politics among Nations.* Boston: McGraw-Hill.
Murphy, Mark (2001) *Natural Law and Practical Rationality.* Cambridge: Cambridge University Press.
Needham, Joseph (1954) *Science and Civilisation in China.* Cambridge: Cambridge University Press.
Oppy, Graham (2012) "Arguments of the Existence of God" in *The Oxford Handbook of Medieval Philosophy.* Marenbon (ed.) Oxford: Oxford University Press, pp. 687–704.
Oslington, Paul (ed.) (2011) *Adam Smith as Theologian.* New York: Routledge.
Parson, Talcott (1951) *The Social System.* Glencoe, IL: The Free Press.
Phillips, Richard Percival (1935) *Modern Thomistic Philosophy: An Explanation for Students*, Vol. II. London: Burns, Oates & Washbourne.
Pieper, Josef (1960) *Scholasticism: Personalities and Problems of Medieval Philosophy.* South Bend, IN: St Augustine's Press.
Quine, Willard (1980) "Two Dogmas of Empiricism" in *From a Logical Point of View.* London: Harvard University Press.
Raff, Rudolf (1996) *The Shape of Life: Genes, Development and the Evolution of Animal Form.* Chicago: University of Chicago Press.

Reid, Thomas (2005) *The Works of Thomas Reid*, Vol. 1. Edinburgh: McLachlan & Stewart.
Roland, Jeffery (2014) "On Naturalism in the Quinean Tradition" in *Philosophical Methodology: The Armchair or the Laboratory?* Haug (ed.) London: Routledge.
Rosemann, Philipp (2004) *Peter Lombard*. Oxford: Oxford University Press.
Ross, David (2002) *The Right and the Good*. Oxford: Oxford University Press.
Schumpeter, Joseph A. (1954) *A History of Economic Analysis*. Elizabeth Booty Schumpeter (ed.) Oxford: Oxford University Press.
Scotus, John Duns (1949) *The De Primo Principio of John Duns Scotus*. Translation by Roche. Louvain: The Franciscan Institute.
Shaffer, Jonathan (2003) "Is There a Fundamental Level?" *Nous*, Vol. 37, No. 3, pp. 498–517.
Smith, Craig (2012) "Adam Smith and Natural Law" in *Natural Law, Economics, and the Common Good*. Gregg and James (eds). Exeter: Academic Imprint, pp. 24–37.
Sorell, Thomas (1996) *Descartes*. Oxford: Oxford University Press.
Spinoza, Baruch (1998) *Principles of Cartesian Philosophy*. Indianapolis: Hackett Publishing.
Strawson, Peter (2006) *Individuals: An Essay in Descriptive Metaphysics*. London: Routledge.
Stevenson, Leslie (2004) *Ten Theories of Human Nature*. Oxford: Oxford University Press.
Suarez, Francisco (1964) *Metaphysical Disputation 6*. Translation by Ross. Milwaukee: Marquette University Press.
Suarez, Francisco (1994) *Metaphysical Disputations 17–19*. Translation by Freddoso. New Haven: Yale University Press.
Suarez, Francisco (2004) *Metaphysical Disputations 28–29*. Translation by Doyle. South Bend, IN: St Augustine's Press.
Suarez, Francisco (2007) *Metaphysical Disputation 7*. Translation by Vollert. Milwaukee: Marquette University Press.
Thorndike, Lynn (1923) *History of Magic and Experimental Science, Vol. 1: The First Thirteen Centuries*. New York: Columbia University Press.
Vattel, Emer de (2008) *The Law of Nations*. Indianapolis: Liberty Fund.
Vorobej, Mark (2006) *A Theory of Argument*. Cambridge: Cambridge University Press.
Waldron, Arthur (2012) "China, Natural Law and Economics: The *Discourses on Salt and Iron*" in *Natural Law, Economics, and the Common Good*. Gregg and James (eds). St Andrews Studies in Philosophy and Public Affairs. Exeter: Academic Imprint, pp. 38–64.
Weber, Marianne (1926) *Max Weber*. Tubingen: J.C.B. Mohr.

Weber, Max (1946) *From Max Weber: Essays in Sociology*. Gerth and Mills (eds and trans). New York: Oxford University Press.
West-Eberhard, Mary Jane (2003) *Developmental Plasticity and Evolution*. New York: Oxford University Press.
Williams, Bernard (1978) *Descartes: The Project of Pure Enquiry*. London: Penguin.
Wilson, Margaret (1991) *Descartes*. London: Routledge.
Winer, Benjamin James (1971) *Statistical Principles in Experimental Design*, 2nd ed. New York: McGraw-Hill.
Woods, Thomas (2015) *How the Catholic Church Built Western Civilization*. Washington, DC: Regnery History.
Wordsdorfer, Manuel (2013) "On the Economic Ethics of Walter Eucken," in *60 Years of Social Market Economy. Formation, Development and Perspectives of a Peace-Making Formula*. Konrad Adenauer Stiftung (ed.). Sankt Augustin, pp. 21–42.
Wulf, Maurice de (1909) *History of Medieval Philosophy*. New York: Longmans, Green & Co.
Yandell, Keith (2005) *Philosophy of Religion: A Contemporary Introduction*. London: Routledge.

INDEX

Abelard, Peter 74, 87, 91, 161, 185
  rules for resolving contradictions from *Sic et Non* 91–2
Albertus Magnus 51, 74
Alexander of Hales 74
Anscombe, Elizabeth 150
Anselm of Canterbury 74, 185
aporetic method 75–7, 81–4, 124
aporia 10, 12, 13, 15, 18, 19, 23
  problem of change 28, 39–41
    non-scholastic solutions 41–2
    scholastic solution 42–4
      as a pre-condition of the sciences 46
  problem of universals 28, 30–3
    non-scholastic solutions 33–5
    scholastic solution 35–9
      as a pre-condition of the sciences 46
Aquinas, Thomas 3, 38, 70, 74, 78, 94, 95, 100, 111–13, 125–8, 130, 131, 141, 153, 158, 162, 165, 166, 167, 170, 171, 172, 185, 186, 187, 188
  cosmological argument (second way) 112, 125–30, 131
  theory of practical reason 141–4, 170–2
    applied to Weberian disenchantment 145–8
Aristotle 3, 27, 32, 35, 36, 37, 42, 44, 60, 64, 73–8, 81–9, 94, 112, 122, 128, 129, 142, 156, 157, 158, 162–8, 170, 171, 185, 186
Augustine 3, 50, 184
Avicenna 131, 132, 185

Bacon, Roger 50, 51
Bonaventure 74
Boscovich, Roger 52
Brucker, Johann 70
Buridan, John 3

Cajetan 3, 187
causation 58–67, 126
  causal powers and liabilities 61, 63–4, 67
Cavalieri, Francesco 52
Chalmers and the zombie argument 107–8
common sense ix, 10, 23, 24, 26–44, 46, 62, 69, 84, 87, 111, 120, 142, 158, 167, 174, 175
  what counts as a common sense belief 29–30

condemnations of 1277 84–7, 98, 103, 105, 163, 164, 175, 186
Cousin, Victor 70

Democritus 43, 157
Descartes, Rene 27, 28, 71, 75, 86, 87, 107, 110, 162, 163, 166, 175, 188, 189
  on method 77–84, 175
  on the real distinction of mind and body 104–6
distinctions x, 112, 149, 165, 166, 175, 176
  cultural importance of 89–91
  essential distinction defined 97
  formal distinction defined 99
  major real distinction defined 97
  as a means of resolving contradictions 91–6
  mental distinction defines 98
  minor real distinction defined 97
  modal distinction defined 100
    knowledge of distinctions 101–3
      post-scholastic criterion: conceivability as guide to real distinction 103, 104, 107, 108, 131, 166
      scholastic criterion: actuality as guide to real distinction 102
Duhem, Pierre 12, 47, 48, 53, 54, 55, 57, 58, 66–7, 122, 154, 158. *See also* Quine, Willard van Orman, Quine-Duhem hypothesis

essentialism 42–4, 175
Eucken, Walter 145, 172

fact-value distinction 24, 139, 140, 176

Galileo, Galilei 48, 159, 188
Gellner, Ernest 15, 154
Giles of Rome 74
globalization 18–20, 138
Grice, Paul 55–7, 61, 64, 160
Grimaldi Francesco 52
Grossteste, Robert 51
Grotius, Hugo 87, 189

Hawking, Stephen 4
Henry of Ghent 74
Heraclitus 27, 43
Hobbes, Thomas 70, 189
human predicament, the 13–15
Hume, David 25–6, 85, 160, 166, 189
  on causation 58–67, 124
hylomorphism 36–9

John of Salisbury 74

Kant, Immanuel 43, 52, 130, 189
  on causation 58–67
Kircher, Athanius 52

Leibniz, Gottfried 86, 115, 162, 188, 189
  Leibniz's Law 40, 42, 105, 106
Lessius, Leonardus 52

Macelwane, J. B 52
meta-philosophy 27, 89, 164
  characterisation of philosophical questions 6–13 (*see also* aporia)
  components of 70–1 (*see also* aporetic method; Descartes, Rene, on method)

Mlodinov, Leonard 4
modernity 2, 48, 183, 184, 188
 aporia arising from social order of modernity 18–23
  scholastic response to these aporia 141–52
 characterisation of 16–17
 crises of 17, 136, 155, 169
Molina, Luis de 51
Moore, G. E. 25, 27, 28, 29–30, 39, 52, 139, 141, 176
 Open Question Argument x, 108–10, 139, 149, 170, 176
moral scepticism and anti-realism, arguments for 139–41
 scholastic responses 148–52

naturalism 108, 113, 116, 117, 120–5, 130, 132, 188
Newton, Newtonian microphysicalism 53, 114, 115, 189
Nicolas of Autrecourt 85, 163–4, 186
Nietzsche, Frederick 22, 150

Ockham, William 3, 38, 70, 100, 158, 186
Odenbach, Frederick 52
Oppy, Graham and standards of argument evaluation 116–20
Oresme, Nicole 51

Parmenides 27, 40, 41
Parsons, Talcott 154, 155
Plato 27, 35, 43, 157

Quine, Willard van Orman 130
 Quinean naturalism 122–4
 Quine-Duhem hypothesis 53–5, 57–8, 67

redundancy thesis, the vii, ix, 1–6, 174
 critique drawn from scientific domain 6–13
 critique drawn from social order 13–23
Reid, Thomas 25, 27, 28, 29, 46, 54
Ricciole, Giambattista 52

scholasticism
 formal characterisation 71–5
 at home in the real world 23–4
 key figures of 74
 meta-philosophy of (*see* aporetic method; distinctions)
 preliminary characterisation 2–3
School of Salamanca 145, 172, 188
Schumpeter, Joseph 156, 159, 172
Sciences, the
 design of scientific experiments 57–67
 emergence of 47–55
 pre-conditions of 49–67, 145
Scotus, John Duns 3, 95, 96, 97, 99, 100, 111, 112, 113, 130, 158, 165, 186
 modal version of the ontological argument 112, 130–3 (*see also* distinctions, formal distinction defined)
Shaffer, Johnathan 114, 115, 126
Smith, Adam 145, 190
social order
 aporia arising from the social order of modernity 18–23, 136–9

basic features of any social order 15–16
basic features of modernity 16–18
legitimacy of 17, 19, 22, 24, 136–9, 151, 176
Spinoza, Baruch 43, 189
Steno, Nicholas 51
Suarez, Francisco 3, 38, 89, 91, 166, 188
on the various kinds of distinction 96–101

Tolstoy, Leo 22

Vitoria, Francisco 3, 87, 188

Weber, Max 9, 16, 21, 22, 155
Weberian disenchantment x, 9, 21, 24, 135–52, 155, 169, 176
William of Conches 51
Wittgenstein, Ludwig 8

Zucchie, Nicolas 52